Tips for
Teams

WITHDRAWN

Tips for Teams

A Ready Reference for Solving Common Team Problems

Kimball Fisher
Steven Rayner
William Belgard
and the
Belgard • Fisher • Rayner Team

James Armstrong
Kathleen Braun
Barbara Brenneman
Mark Christensen
Susanne Eaton
Sheri Piercy
Bonnie Sabel

McGraw-Hill, Inc.

New York   San Francisco   Washington, D.C.   Auckland   Bogotá
Caracas   Lisbon   London   Madrid   Mexico City   Milan
Montreal   New Delhi   San Juan   Singapore
Sydney   Tokyo   Toronto

Library of Congress Cataloging-in-Publication Data

Fisher, Kimball
   Tips for teams : a ready reference for solving common team
problems / Kimball Fisher, Steven Rayner, William Belgard.
       p.   cm.
     ISBN 0-07-021167-1.—ISBN 0-07-021224-4 (pbk.)
     1. Work groups. 2. Problem solving. 3. Conflict management.
   I. Rayner, Steven R. II. Belgard, William. III. Title.
   HD66.F563 1995
   658.4'02—dc20   94-21376
                                                                     CIP

2 3 4 5 6 7 8 9 0   DOC/DOC   9 0 9 8 7 6 5 4   (HC)
2 3 4 5 6 7 8 9 0   DOC/DOC   9 0 9 8 7 6 5 4   (PBK)

ISBN 0-07-021224-4 (HC)
ISBN 0-07-021167-1 (PB)

*The sponsoring editor for this book was Philip Ruppel, the editing
supervisor was Fred Dahl, and the production supervisor was
Pamela Pelton. It was set in Antiqua by Inkwell Publishing Services.*

Printed and bound by R. R. Donnelley & Sons Company.

To our families and friends

Contents

Part Two: Team Tools and Procedures

Foreword

This is a book about teams written by a team. We used many of the tips listed here ourselves as we worked through the problems associated with writing this book together. It wasn't always easy. More on this later.

The coauthors work at Belgard • Fisher • Rayner (BFR) alliance companies. Although we have all worked in high performance work teams as team leaders or team members we do have diverse backgrounds and experiences. We have worked in companies like Procter & Gamble, Tektronix, and Hewlett-Packard, as well as in other organizations like restaurants, postal services, and the U.S. Navy. We have a broad range of educational backgrounds as well, ranging from limited university experience to graduate degrees and postgraduate studies. We don't all live in the same state and our work requires that we travel frequently all over the world, making it difficult for us to communicate regularly.

To further complicate matters, we are all pretty opinionated and head strong. We all wondered whether this project could really be done by a team like us. Writing a book as a team would require us to collaborate closely and make and implement hundreds of joint decisions. That's tough to do when you don't see each other very often.

Nevertheless, we decided to do it. In spite of the challenges we faced we shared a passion for this work. The whole focus of our work is to help organizations implement empowerment. We want more than anything else to help people make their teams effective. So when McGraw-Hill approached us about this project we decided to give it a try despite what seemed to be an almost impossible timeline given our already rigorous work commitments.

We thought we would start by using the same process we recommend to our clients. We used some of the BFR Team Tools™ training modules to help us establish our team charter and some operating guidelines for this project. Frankly, most of us thought this was an unnecessary use of our precious, limited time. After all we are experts on teams. We had written these training materials. Certainly this kind of process was unnecessary for people of our experience. We were wrong. The start-up process helped. It served to clarify unclear roles and responsibilities and resolved some immediate concerns. Teammates, for example, had questions about the priority of this project relative to other work assignments. There were concerns about who was best qualified to write which sections. Some team members with less writing experience wanted to contribute to the book in a meaningful way but expressed reluctance about taking writing tasks. We had an extended debate about how the second part of the book should look until Steve Rayner put the issue to rest by volunteering to write highlights of materials he and Mark Christensen had written for other BFR training programs. I volunteered to edit the completed book.

During the start-up I was appointed team leader. In this role I coordinated the activities with the publisher and developed a sample format for the book. I distributed our book proposal and other correspondence to the team along with the book outline and samples. Completing the process, the team developed a charter, operating guidelines, and a project plan with timeframes.

Like many products written by teams, the charter and guidelines were composed of long compound sentences which represented hours of active debate, some compromising and eventual consensus. Left undone at that time was the specific work assignments. Some people volunteered for writing, formatting, or proofreading sections of the book, but most said they would do whatever was needed. The team asked me to make up final assignments incorporating the tasks for which people had already volunteered. In subsequent meetings those assignments and the project timeline were agreed to by the team.

So far so good. By the end of these first few activities people felt good. The training helped to solidify us as a team. There was a clear direction, we each knew what we were expected to do, we liked the way the project was organized, and everyone expressed a willingness to support our agreements.

The early excitement developed by the start-up process, however, was soon replaced by the uncomfortable realization that the deadlines were looming rapidly upon us. Although everyone had agreed to the timelines, only half of the team finished their research assignments on time. The second deadline (each writer completing one of the problem statements for early editorial review) was missed by everyone. Things began to get a little sweaty. I began giving gentle reminders of our commitments in team meetings. Over time the reminders became less gentle. Directly during the heaviest scheduled writing time, BFR consultants were awarded several new contracts. Because of our values around serving customers, the book took a back seat. To further complicate matters a large portion of the writing that had been completed was trapped on an unreadable computer disk that had been damaged somehow during one of Steve's travels. The time for the completion of the tips came and went with only about 40 percent of the assignments completed.

Wondering if we could meet the original commitments, I began to send out frantic E-mail notes, faxes, and letters. Although there were legitimate reasons for the delays, we had promised our publisher a book. And no one was willing to send out a second-rate job. With only a few weeks left, how was the team going to get the work done?

Well, the short answer was that we found a way. Like other high-performance teams we had worked with, team members got the job done. Late hours, weekends, and shifting responsibilities were required. Team members gave up portions of their holiday time. Families provided support way above and beyond the call of duty. *Tips for Teams* was finished within a few days of the original schedule.

We wrote the reference guide as a team and it is better than the product that any one of us could have developed alone. We witnessed in those last few days the miracle of high-performance work team synergy. We saw the flexibility and commitment that can occur with these work structures of the future. It reminded us again of why we chose this line of work. We hope you will find our effort as helpful to you as it was to our team to create it.

Kimball Fisher
Beaverton, Oregon

Preface

This book is a problem-solving guide for everyone who is on a team. Why a book about solving team problems?

Thousands, perhaps hundreds of thousands, of teams have sprung up across the business and government horizon in the last five years. These participative groups are rapidly becoming the new mainstay of contemporary organizations. It is no longer unusual to hear reports of teams accomplishing improvements which are 30 to 50 percent better than similar, more traditional non-team based organizations.

However, these teams clearly have their own unique set of challenges. We are reminded of the story of a wise man who was once confronted by a frustrated business manager burdened with many personal and business problems. The manager asked the wise man why he had been singled out with this terrible burden. After a few minutes of silent thought, the wise man said he couldn't answer the manager's question. But he told him that he knew of a group of people who had no problems at all. He asked the manager if he would like to meet them. Thinking that these unique individuals might have some suggestions for him, the manager eagerly accepted the wise man's invitation. Following the lead of the wise man the manager walked down the street for some distance. Before long the wise man turned a corner and walked through the gates of their destination. It was a graveyard.

Everyone has problems. They are a natural part of our lives. It doesn't matter what kind of high performance work teams you use; self-directed teams or project teams, permanent natural work group teams or temporary cross-functional teams, factory teams, office teams, unionized teams or management teams. How do you make a team decision when people strongly disagree? How do you deal with sticky personal issues with a fellow team member? What do you do when team meetings seem like a waste of time? How do you handle people who don't want to be part of the team? What do you do if people don't implement the team decision? What if the team leader doesn't "walk the talk"? How can the team leader help without inappropriately dominating the team? These and other types of problems must be solved if teams are going to survive and prosper. And every problem solved together successfully makes the team stronger and more self-reliant.

This book will provide some tips for these and more than a hundred additional problems commonly faced by teams today. Some suggestions will help you steer clear of avoidable problems in the first place. It summarizes the learnings from hundreds of teams in companies like Corning, Apple Computers, AT&T, Kodak, Weyerhaeuser, Motorola, Rockwell, and others and is grounded in the latest research on team effectiveness.

How Is the Guide Organized?   The book is divided into two parts. In the first part, the book reviews common problems and suggests how to solve them. The second part is a reference resource of checklists, processes, and techniques for teams.

The first part of the book includes six sections with common problems or opportunities listed in each section. The sections build progressively on each other as described in what we call the "seashell model" (see Fig. P.1).

After dealing with common cultural problems that form the foundation for teams (Section One), the book progresses to problems with individual team members (Section Two), problems with teams (Section Three), problems between teams (Section Four), problems across the enterprise (Section Five), and problems outside of the organization, especially with customers and vendors (Section Six). Each problem or

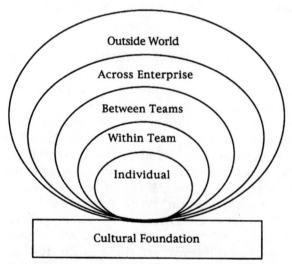

Figure P.1. The seashell model: how *Tips* is organized.

issue statement is followed by two to five suggested tips. These tips make frequent references to the processes and techniques in the second part of the book. In this way the first part of the book serves as an index to the 21 general decision-making and problem-solving tools listed in the second part.

How Should This Guide Be Used? We hope that this format will be user-friendly. Rather than laboring through an academic sounding encyclopedia of team issues, you will turn to a recognizable problem and be guided to other appropriate references. Like a medical reference guide indexed by patient symptoms rather than complicated medical terms, this book is intended to be a practical tool. It is a reference guide that will help you resolve the typical and predictable problems associated with working in teams.

Remember to look at several problem statements which are similar to the problem you are trying to address. There may be a number of useful tips in those sections that will help you. Sometimes the same tip will be repeated under several problem statements. This normally means that these tips are particularly helpful in a variety of situations. Please read the dozen tips in the introduction. They will be useful in resolving nearly every problem your team will run into.

The tips in this guide will not always be the specific answers to your problems. Each situation is different. Carefully evaluate the tips only as suggestions, rather than as prescriptions, for your issues. Only you and your team can decide what is best to do in your unique situation. Also, remember that some of the tips listed in this guide may fall outside of your current area of responsibility. *If any tip you read is outside of your boundary conditions, or feels uncomfortable to you, get some help from your team leader, senior management, or human resources representative.* Don't do anything outside of your current boundary conditions without renegotiating with your leadership.

In summary, in the midst of a glut of information about why teams are so important, team members still have little help to get them through the normal day-to-day problems that besiege them. That is why we wrote *Tips for Teams*. It certainly isn't a panacea for all team problems. You must thoughtfully consider the unique characteristics of your situation and do what is appropriate. But it is our sincere wish that you will find this a practical and useful tool which will trigger your own creative juices and make you think of alternative ways to resolve your team problems. We sincerely hope that you and your team will achieve everything you want to accomplish.

Acknowledgments. We are indebted to a number of scholars and practitioners for their work on the subject of teams and high performance work systems. In particular we have drawn from the work of Eric Trist, Marvin Weisbord, Edwards Deming, Jack Sherwood, Pam Posey, Jan Klein, Richard Walton, Len Schlesinger, Ed Lawler, James Schonk, Steve Covey, Peter Senge, Peter Scholtes, William Byham, Bob Harper, Ann Harper, Mark Kelly, Richard Wellins, Lawrence Miller, Jon Katzenbach, Douglas Smith, BFR associates Mareen Fisher, Phil Bromley and Mike Hunter, our affiliates in the London Practick office, Ronan Knox, Geoffrey Peppiatt, Rodney Drew and others like Bill Lytle, Jack Zenger, Ed Musselwhite, Bruce Dillingham, Ralph Stayer, Lyman Ketchum, and Stu Winby who have worked to make these important topics so accessible and practical. We have drawn heavily from ideas in Steven Rayner's *Recreating the Work Place* (Oliver Wight, 1993) and from Kimball Fisher's *Leading Self-Directed Work Teams* (McGraw-Hill, 1993) as well as from a number of other articles from Fisher and Rayner, including materials published by Belgard • Fisher • Rayner, Inc.

We acknowledge the work of our fellow team members who authored this guide. James Armstrong wrote tips on resistance to teams, performance, skills and training, and external issues; William Belgard wrote tips on coping with change, focus and purpose, and corporate management and policies; Kathleen Braun wrote tips on meetings, decision making, celebrations and she helped format Section Two, Barbara Brenneman did proofreading, mailings, and data entry; Mark Christensen was the primary author of the BFR Team Tools™ training program on which most of Section Two is based; Susanne Eaton wrote the tips on interpersonal problems, Kimball Fisher wrote the tips on team design and structure, team leader problems, book forematter, introduction, selected additional tips, and he edited Section One; Sheri Piercy facilitated team communications and did proofreading and data entry; Steven Rayner wrote tips on communication, problems between teams, organized labor and management, pay concerns, edited Section Two, and helped write the " ® Team Tools and BFR Leader Skills™" training program; and Bonnie Sabel wrote tips on individual problems. We especially thank Belgard • Fisher • Rayner, Inc. for the permission to publish highlights from the "BFR Team Tools™ and BFR Leader Skills™" training programs (© 1989-1993, Belgard • Fisher • Rayner, Inc., all rights reserved) in Section Two of this book. BFR Team Tools™ is a modular skill-building program for teams and Leader Skills is a program which clarifies the new role for team leaders in team-based organizations and helps them to become more competent as leaders.

We also wish to thank the professional organizations and associations with whom we have enjoyed especially supportive and educational relationships including the Association of Quality and Participation, the Ecology of Work Conferences, the Institute for International Research, National Technological University, Oliver Wight, Productivity, the Socio-Technical System Roundtable, the University of North Texas Center for the Study of Work Teams, and the Work in America Institute. Our editor and publisher, Philip Ruppel, deserves special credit for his much needed support, encouragement, and flexibility. We also appreciate Rose Kernan of Inkwell Publishing Services for her editing skill.

We are especially grateful to our clients and business associates who have allowed us to learn from some of the best business team examples in the world. Special thanks to Apple Computer, AT&T, Corning, Goodyear, Hewlett-Packard, IBM, Kodak, Monsanto, Motorola, Procter and Gamble, Quaker Oats, Rockwell, Shell, Teccor, and Weyerhaeuser, for showing us tips in action.

We cannot express enough gratitude, of course, to our friends and families who have supported us during the development of this book. Their personal example of support during the holiday season when we were trying to finish our work on *Tips* does much more than warrant the dedication of this book—it inspires us to want to be the best kind of people and team members we can become.

The Belgard • Fisher • Rayner Team

Tips for Teams

Introduction

A Dozen Tips for Everybody Who Works on Teams

Perhaps you have heard the story about an old village with a large beautiful bell located in the middle of town. The village was nestled in the foothills of a great mountain range, and the cliffs acted like a stone amphitheater, which carried the bells dulcet tones far and wide across the village and its neighboring farms. The villagers were very proud of their sweet sounding landmark, and they found several occasions each month to ring it long and cheerfully. But after generations of melodious service, gradually the bell began to sound differently. Instead of the bright pinging tones the villagers had grown to love, the bell made only dull thudding noises. With great concern, the villagers searched for someone to fix their bell. After many months they located an authority on large antique bells who agreed to travel to the village to try to restore their cherished village treasure.

When the bell expert arrived, a small crowd of villagers welcomed her and led her to the town square, where the bell had been lowered from the bell tower onto wooden blocks. The expert walked around the bell slowly. After five minutes of inspection she produced a small wooden mallet from her travel case and tapped the bell. It was fixed. When the bell was hoisted to its tower, it sounded as sweet and beautiful as ever before.

The expert presented the mayor with a bill for $500. Although the mayor was grateful to have the bell fixed, he thought the bill was extravagant. "My," he said, "if your charge for five minutes of work is $500 you must charge $6000 an hour! How can you do that?" "Mayor," replied the expert "the charge for five minutes of work to tap the bell is only $20. The other $480 is for knowing where to tap."

Teams with problems are somewhat like that broken bell. Their potential is temporarily muted until the problems are resolved. There are many helpful tips listed in this book. But more often than not, people who are experienced with teams know, like the bell expert, that there are a few predictable places to tap the team which will fix a disproportionate share of the problems. Our experience with some of the best business teams in North America and Western Europe, for example, has shown us that there are a few things great teams do regularly to solve or avoid problems. A dozen special tips, in particular, are so common in effective teams that we wanted to list them in this introduction. These are the best places to start when solving team problems. If you keep them in mind, they will help you with most of the issues listed here. If done regularly, they will prevent many problems from ever occurring.

Tip 1. Be patient and caring with your team.

Remember to be patient and caring with each other as you work through your problems together. Teams are like families. They are composed of individuals who each have their own special skills, perspectives, and challenges. Be supportive. Reduce status differentials that make some team members seem more important than others. Eliminate inappropriate titles, special treatments, or perquisites based on class or rank. Treat everyone fairly. You'll measure your accomplishments in a series of small improvements, often feeling as though you take three steps forward and then two steps back, seemingly losing your hard won ground. More often than not, it is simple perseverance that determines the difference between the winners and the losers. No one ever said teams are easy. But they are usually better than the alternatives.

Tip 2. Assume the best about people.

You will find that precious few problems are caused intentionally by carelessness or deviousness. Sometimes in our frustrations with the extra headaches caused by these problems, however, we start to assume that others we work with are lazy, or mean, or stupid. This is very counterproductive. More than anything else, the move to team-based organizations requires a paradigm shift. In other words, the way we think about work and the way we think about each other is the main thing that has to change, not organization charts and job descriptions.

When we hear comments about how the night shift always causes problems, or how only managers are supposed to make decisions, or how the union executives are trying to break the back of the company, etc., we are not likely going to see the improvements we desire. These kinds of assumptions will get in the way of teamwork. They cause people to want to defend their points of view and fight to win for their side of the argument. They make it hard to sit down and work things out together. Good problem solving has to start from a foundation of mutual trust and a common desire to improve. Even though it is true that there are a few malicious people around, the vast majority of us share the common goal of wanting our teams to succeed. Effective teams rise above their differences and focus instead on common ground. Assume that the problems you see were caused by good people doing the best they could with the information, systems, and skills they had at the time. Then work to improve information, systems and skills. In particular, focus on creating good real-time information systems. Without them, teams can't make good decisions.

Tip 3. Fix the problem, don't fix the blame.

Experience shows that blaming doesn't solve problems; it just causes them to go underground. When people believe that discussing problems will cause them embarrassment or affect their career negatively, they will not discuss the problem. The road to continuous improvement requires "open and honest communication." The key to that is to avoid blaming and focus instead on solving the problem at hand.

Tip 4. Focus on behaviors, not attitudes.

You can't change other people's personalities and attitudes. But if you work together, you can help each other demonstrate effective behaviors. Remember this when working with others and giving them feedback. Be specific and focus on the real things people say and do. Don't say, "You make me mad" or "You're lazy." There is nothing people can do about those kinds of comments. Instead say, "When you talk to people about my work performance without talking to me about it first it makes me angry," or "When you leave work without cleaning up your project area, that means I have to do the work you left and my work too." These comments help people know what they can do to make an improvement and set the stage for working through the issue.

Tip 5. Establish regular, effective team meetings.

Most problems teams run into will come from miscommunication. To avoid many of the problems mentioned in this reference guide, establish a regular time and place for team meetings. Use these meeting times to pass along information, clarify who is supposed to do what, update each other on your assignments, check progress toward your goals, and just take some time to talk with each other. Have information infrastructures that provide you with up-to-date business information. Create a team climate that fosters frequent, open, and honest discussion where people can share their feelings and learning without fear.

Tip 6. Focus on the race, not the hurdles.

Although your team must learn how to resolve problems successfully, avoid getting caught in an endless downward spiral of problem solving. Just as there are many obstacles on the track of a high hurdle race, there are many problems in the way of effective team-based operations. Staying too focused on an individual hurdle can make you lose the race. Too much focus on problems can be discouraging, depressing, and distracting. Teams keep motivation high by maintaining their focus on the end goal, not by draining their enthusiasm in an endless series of difficulties. Keep your heads up. Effective teams are purpose-oriented rather than problem-solving-oriented. They renew their energy and commitment by keeping their eye on their mission and by not allowing their normal day-to-day frustrations to slow them down. They celebrate their victories, encourage each other regularly, and maintain their team spirit by reminding themselves about the overall race, even when all they can see are the seemingly endless parade of hurdles.

Tip 7. Involve the right people in problem solving.

People are most committed to implementing ideas that they personally participate in developing. Remember this when you decide who should be involved in solving team problems. Does this mean that every problem needs to be solved by the whole team? No. Many can and should be delegated to a subgroup, individual, or team leader.

Tip 8. Don't break your pick on unsolveable problems.

Serious problems should be resolved immediately before they grow into monumental issues requiring extreme measures. Some problems, however, can't be resolved at all, and continual discussion will simply aggravate injuries, which will distract your team from running the race the best they can. Some problems are best ignored and will resolve themselves over time as the team progresses towards the finish line. Only a skillful and well trained team will know the best course of action. A good team leader will coach the team through these issues successfully.

Tip 9. Develop the skills and discipline of effective problem solving.

Team problem solving is a skill. The tips in this ready reference will provide your team small benefits if you haven't properly diagnosed the problem, or if you ignore other elements of effective problem solving. If your team isn't experienced in this, you may want to start by reviewing the sections on problem solving in Part Two of this book before going through the specific tips. See Resource 10: Team Problem Solving and Resource 11: Tools for Problem Solving. Don't worry if you find, as most teams do, that these methods seem a little awkward at first. As your team matures and you regularly practice using these types of methods, you will begin to find that they feel more natural over time. Just keep at it. It's like riding a bicycle.

Tip 10. Know your roles, purpose, boundaries, and resources.

Many problems result from a lack of clarity about what you are supposed to do and how much help you will get to do it. Strive to understand your task as a team and as a team member or team leader. Understand your new roles and responsibilities. Team-based organizations have fundamentally different assignments. If you don't understand these roles, get some help from your team leader, senior manager or training coordinator.

Understanding these things will keep you focused on results and customers, not on activities and busywork. And once that is clear in your mind, get agreements from the appropriate people about your purpose. Don't assume that, if other people don't say anything, they agree with you. Vocalize agreements to ensure mutual understanding. Good questions to ask when you are developing these performance agreements are "How will we know if we have successfully completed this work?" and "What boundaries are we working with as far as time, money, and customer requirements?"

Tip 11. Focus on results.

Remember to stay focused on results. Don't get off track. Avoid the temptation to get swept up in the day-to-day tyranny of the urgent. It can be easy to get carried away with lots of activities, or bound up in lots of programs, red tape, or bureaucracy that don't actually produce results. Keep thinking about your goals. Talk about customers. Create a solid information system infrastructure that will tell you how you are doing on your results on a regular basis. Post this information where people can see it and use this data to make better team decisions. Measure key result areas. Get good results in quality, cost, responsiveness, timeliness, or whatever your team and team leader agree are the overarching purpose of your organization.

Tip 12. Remember that the team is not an end in itself.

Teams are a means to accomplishing something, not an end in themselves. Measure ends, not means. Instead of measuring how many teams you have, measure your results. Instead of asking how to make things more comfortable for the team, ask how to deliver better service to the customer. If your team becomes too inwardly focused, it will not survive. It doesn't matter how good your team is if you don't have products and services that customers are willing to pay for. Meet their needs. People will be happier, and many team problems will dissolve if your operation is successful. People like to be on a winning team. Keeping these dozen tips in mind will save you hours and hours of unnecessary frustration. It is our hope that you never have any problems with your team at all. But since problems are as inevitable as death and taxes, in the following pages of this guide we've prepared some more tips for you on how you and your team might be able to solve them together.

Part One

Common Team Problems

One

Cultural Problems

Problems Affecting the Organization's Receptivity to Teams

Category: Resistance to Teams
Problem: Misunderstanding Teams

Tip 1. Go visit some successful team-based organizations and talk to other people about their experience. Prepare well beforehand to make the most of the visit by developing questions that will get the information necessary to help people understand teams.

Tip 2. Go to conferences where people from team-based organizations are making presentations. Look for conferences where you can hear a variety of teams discussed.

Tip 3. Use specific examples of good teams and explain how things will be different in a team-based organization. You might say:

> At one company we visited, they had great teams. Manufacturing worked so closely with the engineers that they asked us for input when they designed new products to make them easier to manufacture. I think we'll be able to get the engineers to do the same thing here.

It is a good idea to have examples that are not sports related. Many people have not participated in organized sports and may not be able to relate to these examples.

Tip 4. Form team study groups. Have members of the teams commit to find an article, case study, or book about teams and develop a brief report to deliver to the study group. Focus the reports on two key questions:

- What are the key points in the book, article, or case study?
- How can the key points specifically be applied to your situation?

Tip 5. Learn about different types of teams. People are often confused because they think there is only one type of team. There are different types of teams that can be applied to different sets of circumstances. For instance:

Natural work groups—groups of employees who have responsibility for a process (like the engine of a car; or the customer service of an insurance office), and *ad hoc task forces*—groups of employees who are pulled together to resolve a specific issue (like the re-design of a pay system) and then disband.

Tip 6. Create a team charter, principles, guidelines, and boundaries for a potential team that is familiar to the people you are talking to and use these tools to help explain how a team might work in your organization. Resource 1: Creating a Team Charter and Resource 2: Using Principles, Guidelines, and Boundaries provide examples that will help you do this. You could say:

> I think we should look at how teams could specifically apply to our situation. Let's look at a sample team charter we have developed for the cost accounting group.

See Resource 1: Creating a Team Charter
Resource 2: Using Principles, Guidelines, and Boundaries

Category: Resistance to Teams
Problem: Employee Resistance

Tip 7. Ask coworkers who are resistant to teams to talk to proteam employees from other departments and counterparts in other organizations who have achieved success with teams. You could say:

> I wasn't too sure about this team stuff either, but when I talked to Georgette down at the Dallas office she got me really excited by all of the success her team has had. Why don't you give her a call?

You might want to coach them to ask questions like:

> Georgette, I know you think this team stuff makes sense, but what were some of the specific challenges you had to overcome to make it work for you?

Tip 8. Facilitate a meeting where team members list all the aspects of the best job you have had during your careers. See Resource 9: Facilitating Groups for tips on making sessions like this effective. You could start the exercise by saying:

> All of us, hopefully, have had one job or assignment during our careers that we could call our favorite. What specific things made that job your favorite job?

When the brainstorming is finished it is easy to show how the characteristics of most people's favorite jobs fit into team organizations.

See Resource 9: Facilitating Groups

Tip 9. Ask people to list the advantages and disadvantages of being on a team. There is a good chance they will see for themselves that the advantages of teams outweigh the disadvantages. Prior to the meeting you might ask everyone to prepare by saying:

> I know some of us aren't convinced that teams are the way to go, but we need to at least discuss the issue. Before you come to our next meeting think about teams and make a list of all of the advantages and disadvantages of teams that

you can think of. We'll chart all of these and then discuss the lists.

Tip 10.   Review the business needs for using teams. A good simulation exercise which demonstrates a nonteam based organization and then contrasts it with a team-based organization as part of an orientation training program is an excellent participative way to illustrate this point. Part of this orientation might include representatives from senior management and representatives from labor talking about why teams are important for the success of the organization.

Category: Resistance to Teams
Problem: Management Resistance

Tip 11.   Charter a team of executives to help the entire management team develop the understanding and commitment necessary for the success of your team effort. Use Resource 1: Creating a Team Charter to get the team off to a strong start and ask the team to:

- Learn about empowerment and teams.
- "Catch up" with all of the team things that have happened in the organization so far—both good and bad.
- Develop a "case for change" which describes why teams are important from a business point of view.
- Champion the team concept and communicate its value and importance throughout the organization—especially to all levels of management.
- Help plan and guide the team effort as it unfolds.

Select senior managers who have become champions of the team concept to talk to other managers about their convictions. These presentations will help the skeptical and strengthen the champions as well.

See Resource 1: Creating a Team Charter

Tip 12.   Ask them to give you an opportunity to change their minds. When they give you this opportunity organize a team conference where you will invite executives from suppliers and customers to explain their success stories with teams. When you invite your guests ask them to be completely honest about successes and failures. Use information gathered from Resource 4: Building Customer Relationships and Resource 5: Working with Suppliers to determine who to invite.

The last conference activity should be an open discussion by members of your management team about teams and how they may or may not apply in your organization. Often, hearing about and discussing potential applications of teams will help build support.

See Resource 4: Building Customer Relationships
Resource 5: Working with Suppliers

Tip 13. Coordinate a management "tour of teams." Identify organizations with successful teams and ask them to provide your management team with a tour of their organization. When you set up the tours ask the hosting organizations to discuss their entire team journey including how the decision was made to implement teams and all of the advantages and disadvantages related to the team effort.

Develop a proposed agenda using Resource 6: Holding Effective Meetings to help develop a mutually agreed upon agenda for the tour. This will help you get what you need out of the tour and help the hosting organizations communicate what they can and cannot deliver during the tour.

See Resource 6: Holding Effective Meetings

Tip 14. Create a forum for team representatives to come and tell other people in the company about their successes. Make these forums genuine opportunities for sharing and learning.

Category: Coping with Change
Problem: Pace Too Slow

Tip 15. Get help from your team leader. Sometimes management will get a team process started and not follow through on critical elements for success. They may not even know they are not being helpful enough unless you tell them. Start with your team leader and review your team charter and boundary conditions with her. Be as specific as possible about support the team needs to fulfill its charter. You might say:

Patricia, we need some help to take this team concept as far as we feel it needs to go. In our charter it says we will be making more decisions, but we have found that we don't have good enough ongoing information to do that well. In our next team meeting will you tell us about the management financial reports you get and help us understand how to use them?

See Resource 1: Creating a Team Charter
See Resource 2: Using Principles, Guidelines, and Boundaries

Tip 16. Declare your concern. Slow team development may come from not being clear on team purpose, a lack of trust, unclear roles, poor communication, diversity being seen as a block rather than a strength, or from a lack of balance between getting the job done and building team relationships. At a team meeting, express your concern that nothing has really changed and ask others if they feel the same way. If so, suggest that the team diagnose and address issues that may be holding them back.

See Resource 14: Building a Collaborative Team Environment

Tip 17. Work with your team leader to determine whether the barrier to faster team progress is only perceived or whether it actually exists. One of the most significant barriers to improvement is that we think nothing can be done whether it is true or not. For perceived barriers such as "I don't think the section head will allow us to make the equipment decision ourselves," you can determine whether this is a real barrier by asking the section head directly. For actual barriers:

- Try to understand why the barrier exists in the first place.
- Determine who you need to work with to eliminate the barrier.
- Describe the consequences of the barrier on your team.
- Describe how to eliminate the negative impact of the barrier.
- Identify what there is to gain or lose by what you are recommending.
- Look for opportunities to have your case heard.

See Resource 21: Barrier Busting

Category: Coping with Change
Problem: Ideas Not Listened To

Tip 18. When management won't listen, review your team's charter and boundary conditions with your team leader. You might say:

> The team is frustrated by a lack of management attention to our ideas and it's keeping us from doing our job. We need to make sure we are working on the right things and that management will listen to us when we come forward with ideas for change. Will you help us do that?

Tip 19. When suppliers won't listen, help them understand how that hurts both of your organizations. Suppliers are any individual or group who provides you with a product or service. For many teams, key suppliers are primarily other groups in your own company. Show them how to listen to you by the way you listen to them. Begin by reviewing with them how what they do is important to your team and what you do. Be clear about why it's important to you that they listen and work closely with you. Ask them to explain how your team is important to them and ask for feedback from them about working with you before giving them feedback yourselves. As you work through this issue, take the opportunity to set up or improve a process for regular feedback between both parties.

See Resource 5: Working with Suppliers
See Resource 8: Giving and Receiving Feedback

Tip 20. When customers won't listen ask for their help. A customer is someone inside or outside your organization to whom you provide products or services. If customers are unwilling or unable to listen to your ideas for change, share your concerns with them, clearly stating the issue and ask for their help to solve it. You might say:

> We think it's our job to help you to be successful and that means helping to make change happen. But when we have ideas to make things better, we don't feel listened to. That keeps us from doing our job. Will you help us learn how best to communicate our ideas to you in ways that can help both of us?

See Resource 4: Building Customer Relationships

Tip 21. If team members won't listen it may be because they do not see their purpose, their roles, or their responsibilities the same way. To confront the issue directly, you might say:

> Something is blocking our ability to listen to (and accept) ideas for change from one another and it's keeping us from doing our job. Let's review our roles and responsibilities to see if we can find the disconnect.

See Resource 13: Team Communication Basics
See Resource 14: Building a Collaborative Team Environment
See Resource 16: Team Member Roles and Responsibilities

Category: Coping with Change
Problem: Unshared Need to Change

Tip 22. Develop a "case for change" with the team, coming to consensus on each of the following questions:

- Why does our organization need to change?
- What will happen if we don't?
- What's in it for all of us if we do?

Discuss these items thoroughly, then post the results and share it with others in your organization.

Tip 23. Review your team charter as a group. This may help refocus energy on change and remind everyone why you're a team in the first place. Highlight the overall purpose of the team, your key customers, and why what you do is important to them. Emphasize the key result areas your team is expected to accomplish, your guiding principles, and time frames.

See Resource 1: Creating a Team Charter

Tip 24. Review your common purpose with the team. Teams that have a shared sense of purpose understand the need for change as it relates to their mission as a team. Discuss why your team exists and why it's important that you be successful. Allow each team member to express commitment. Use your common purpose to prioritize team actions.

See Resource 14: Building a Collaborative Team Environment

Tip 25. Get good business information. Sometimes a lack of a commonly felt need for change comes from a lack of information. Team members and team leaders are more likely to see the need for continuous change when they understand changing customer requirements, competitive situations, and other market pressures. Create a process for communication which allows regularly updated information to be shared with the teams. The best information is firsthand. Visit some customers, for example, rather than only reading about their preferences in marketing reports.

Category: Coping with Change
Problem: Nonnegotiables and Unchangeables

Tip 26. Justify your change idea. If you cannot change something, is there part of it that your sponsoring or direct team leader could change? If so, be specific about how the larger issue blocks the team and what you need from management to help accomplish business improvements. A good approach is to go through a cost/benefits analysis. Determine the cost of the change, determine the amount of the benefit in cost or time savings to your team, and show how the investment is warranted by the return you get from making the change.

See Resource 21: Barrier Busting

Tip 27. Minimize the negative effects of the unchangeable. With the team, clearly state what the issue is and how it negatively affects the work that needs to be done. Brainstorm ways that the team might minimize the impact of the block on the team's performance. Try to get outside the normal "box" of thinking and examine the problem from many angles. Sometimes solutions come from different ways of seeing the problem.

Tip 28. Learn to cope with things you can't change. Sometimes bad things happen to good teams, and there is nothing that you can do but make the best of it. It is said that all things work together for good. Look for ways that, taken together, all that's happening will produce some good. With the team, brainstorm and agree on ways to help and support one another through the tough time. Sometimes, identifying the worst thing that can happen, then planning a way to get through it makes you feel stronger and more confident. If you can't change something, work together to learn how to cope with it.

Tip 29.   Remember that everyone has things they can't change. In team-based organizations some of these are called *boundary conditions*. Boundaries can include things such as money or time. Things outside the boundaries cannot be changed, but things inside the boundaries can change. It is best to know these up front before progressing very far on the task. Once you know what these boundaries are, you can focus your energy on the things you can change within those boundaries.

Category: Coping with Change
Problem: Changing the Unknown

Tip 30.   Say that something is wrong and get the ball rolling, even if you don't exactly know what is wrong. When things begin to go wrong the first signs may be only noticeable to a few people. Declaring your concern early might save bigger problems later. You might say:

> It feels like there is something not quite right here. Does anyone else feel it? I'd like to review some key aspects of our project team and see if we can spot anything. Will you help me do this?

Areas to explore include team purpose, trust, roles, communication, diversity, and balance of task and relationships.

See Resource 14: Building a Collaborative Team Environment

Tip 31.   Deal with conflict. Sometimes things feel wrong when conflict is not being dealt with or identified openly. Some indicators include:

People's personal lives tend to interfere with work or vice versa

People avoid each other

Team members feel blocked by one person

Subgroups are forming

Hard feelings exist

Determine if hidden conflict exists and decide what to do about it.

See Resource 15: Managing Team Conflict

Tip 32. Do an ideal team gap analysis. Declare your concern and share your feelings about how the team is operating right now and ask others to do the same. List together what is happening versus what you want to happen, and look for gaps that may point to the source of the trouble. Together, discuss ways to close the gaps and agree on a process for implementation and follow-up. A good way to do this is to ask team members to visualize what your team would be like if everything was ideal. Write their comments down on a large piece of chart paper. Then go to each written comment and ask the team to write a statement that reflects their current status on that attribute. If one of the ideal statements, for example, is "We treat everybody with dignity and respect," the team may say that the way they currently act is to "Treat technical people with more respect than nontechnical people." Decide what to do about it.

Two

Team Member Problems

Problems That Affect Someone's Ability to Be an Effective Team Member

Category: Individual Team Problems
Problem: Nonteam Players

Tip 33. First, consider whether your own perception of what this person should be doing is correct. Assume that the person has good intent and wants to act like a team player, but just doesn't understand what that means the same way you do. Refer to the team charter and anything else the team developed about how the work will be done. If your teammate is doing what is consistent with your previous agreements, but the work has changed enough to warrant a modification, change the charter, guidelines, or job assignments accordingly. You may also want to suggest that the team review and update the team member responsibilities as mentioned in Resource 16: Team Member Roles and Responsibilities.

See Resource 16: Team Member Roles and Responsibilities

Tip 34. If you try the things in tip 33, but still have problems with your teammate, then remember to talk directly with him about it. Avoid the temptation to discuss it with other team members to see if they agree with you. Think of the golden rule: "Do unto others as you would have them do unto you." If someone thought you weren't doing your job, would you want them discussing it with others, or would you want them to come to you first? Moreover, if you talk to other team members about someone else, they will probably feel you would talk about them behind their back, too. This erodes the trust in the team. Remember to be specific when you talk to your team member. You might say:

> Bob, I don't feel like we are working as well as we can as a team. Last week when we had the big order come in, for example, everyone went over to the warehouse to help out except you. When you stay at your desk at a time like that, it makes me feel like you don't care as much as I do about getting our team results.

Or:

> Bob, when we had our team meeting this morning you didn't volunteer to serve on any of the project teams again. I know you're busy, but I don't feel like you get as involved in our team activities as we need you to. Am I way off base here?

Tell your teammate how you feel. Don't try to explain how everyone else feels, or to become a spokesperson for the whole team. Everyone who has feedback should give it directly to the individual. You may try other things later if this doesn't work, but as a first attempt to help people change, work directly with the individual one-on-one.

Tip 35. When you talk to your teammate, you want to leave them feeling okay as a person. Remember that they may have a perception about their responsibilities that is entirely different from yours, but is equally valid. You might start by saying something like:

> Mary, in our team meeting last week we discussed a new part selection process that we agreed we would all start doing. Is that how you understood it?

Listen to the answer before going ahead. It is possible that your teammate simply misunderstood that she had this responsibility. If she agrees that it is her responsibility, however, briefly identify the behavior that is causing a problem, the results of this behavior on the work, and your feelings. See Resource 8: Giving and Receiving Feedback. For example:

> Mary, when you don't complete this process before sending the parts forms to my station, then I need to do it before I can begin my operation. This causes work to back up at my station, and then I worry that the team may not complete our daily commitment on time.

See Resource 8: Giving and Receiving Feedback
See Resource 16: Team Member Roles and Responsibilities

Tip 36. Avoid blaming people because they may become defensive and resolving the problem will be more difficult. Instead, try to identify the process that is causing a person to act in an undesirable way. Ask open-ended questions (which can't be answered with a "yes" or no) about how the work is currently done, what the person is getting rewarded to do, how the work has changed over time, and so on. Try to pinpoint parts of the systems or processes that need to be modified to improve the problem. The reason someone might be acting more like a loner than a team member, for example, might be that your performance appraisal system focuses on individual accomplishments and not enough on working together as a team. In this case it is unlikely to expect your teammate to change until the performance appraisal system is modified appropriately. Some questions to ask to identify the kinds of things that might need to be changed include things like:

> What gets in the way of you doing your job the best way you can?

> What gets in the way of us working as a team more effectively?

> If you could change something to help us meet our customer needs better, what would you change?

To aid this analysis, consider using some of the problem-solving tools in Resource 11: Tools For Problem Solving. You might use the force-field analysis for this type of situation.

See Resource 11: Tools for Problem Solving

Tip 37. If the particular problem has to do with a team member who does not seem to have the same sense of urgency or willingness to carry their fair share of the load, and you have tried the preceding tips you may have to deal with this as a performance problem. Determine whether a performance problem should be addressed by the team or by management. If it can be addressed by the team, a "Team Performance Board" of four to six members of the team could be chartered by the team to act as a review committee for performance issues. The prime charter of the board would be to help people improve. The board would review performance problem issues and help people develop a "get-well plan" to improve specific behaviors. If the agreed-on plan is not followed by the team member, then the board would recommend disciplinary action (up to and including termination for very serious offenses) to senior management. This would be a formal process, well documented, consistent with agreed-on practices or contracts, and consistently followed. The Human Resources department and union executives would need to help to ensure legality and process integrity. The employee could appeal to senior management if desired.

Category: Individual Team Problems
Problem: Too Busy for Teamwork

Tip 38. Recognize that being a team member takes time. Make sure members know this at start-up and are committed to be available.

Tip 39. Remember that everyone has exactly the same amount of time (24 hours a day) as everyone else. When people don't have time for teamwork they actually believe that the teamwork isn't as high a priority as the other work they do. Try to understand why. Make adjustments so that the teamwork is an appropriate priority. You might have the person list their priorities and check them with the team to see if the team supports the priority list or if they have a different perspective of what is most important to get the customer what is needed.

Tip 40. Ask yourself why this person is too busy. Some possibilities include: Has the team allocated more work to one team member than others? Does this person volunteer to take on too many tasks? Does the team operate in a way that whoever sees something that needs to be done owns the responsibility to do it—and is this a person who sees things that need to be done? Is this person too busy because she does a job too thoroughly? Is this person "too busy" as a way of avoiding interacting with the team? Is team interaction safe, or does it appear risky to this person because of personal preferences or cultural upbringings? Is the person unwilling to interact because he believes his opinions are ignored or devalued? Has this person experienced criticism on the job, making him unwilling to risk the exposure or embarrassment that could come from the possibility of failing on something in front of peers?

When you understand why the person is too busy, take appropriate action.

See Resource 9: Facilitating Groups

Tip 41. Even on teams where team members perform tasks that are quite different and may require different training or experience, every job has elements that are transferable with a small amount of explanation. Try offering some assistance. You might say:

> Sally, I'd like for you to feel you have the time to come to the team meeting, so I'm offering you a half-hour of my time later today to help in any way I can.

If she has taken on too many tasks, discuss it at a team meeting. You might say:

> Sally, we notice you're working longer hours than most of the team, and that sometimes you feel you are too busy for team meetings. We think it's important that you have the same opportunity to participate with the rest of the team, to keep informed and share your contributions with the team. We'd like to work together to identify some of the added tasks you've taken on, and see if the team can help redistribute the work, or if it's possible any of the tasks can be postponed or discontinued so that you will be free to participate more fully.

Tip 42. Sometimes work situations where an employee is, or feels, criticized will cause a person to strive for perfection to avoid further criticism. This can increase the time required to do tasks. Recognizing and verbalizing (rewarding) the behaviors you want to see repeated can be very effective in helping them to relax and feel more accepted. You may want to recognize that some tasks do not need to be completed beyond an "acceptable standard." This will free up time for other things.

Tip 43. Warmly recognize when she does take time to participate on the team. This positive reinforcement is sometimes enough to encourage people to prioritize their own work to spend more time in the team activities they feel good about.

Tip 44. Try asking him directly if something has happened which makes it difficult for him to make the necessary time to work with the team. If so, try to help him resolve it. You might say:

> Ted, I notice that you've been very busy lately, and that you aren't participating in the daily team projects. Did anything happen which makes you want to avoid the team activities?

Remain objective (avoid taking sides or criticizing another team member). Listen and follow up with an offer such as:

> If you would like to talk to John and share how you're feeling, I'd be glad to help you set up a meeting or to let you practice giving the feedback to me if it would help.

You might remind them that you feel their contributions are important to the success of the team.

Tip 45. Try to discover the root cause of the problem. Review the five-step process for team problem solving in Resource 10.

See Resource 10: Team Problem Solving

Category: Individual Team Problems
Problem: Laggards and Deadwood

Tip 46. Find out what happened to cause this problem. If you are working hard and think someone else is not, this can be very disheartening, especially if they enjoy the same rewards as the rest of the team. You will want to understand how this situation came to exist. Ask yourself, whether this person was a hard worker before, and whether or not something has changed? If so, do you know what changed? Could you ask them? Once identified, you may be able to easily address the problem. Remember, however, that everyone has bad days. Before taking additional steps make sure that you are observ-

ing a pattern of behavior and not something unusual that may
be the result of temporary problems at home.

Tip 47. It is always best to genuinely try to help your team
members improve before attempting other measures. The first
step in this improvement process is feedback. She may not
even realize that you don't think she is carrying her fair share
of the workload. Before you give the feedback, however, honestly ask yourself the question, "Am I going to tell my team
member how I feel just so I can get it off my chest, or is it my
intent to help them improve?" If the reason is primarily to
make yourself feel better you will usually not be able to help
someone else.

It is appropriate as a team member to give feedback to
another team member about how the work is getting done (or
not getting done). There is a special way to do this so that it is
most likely to help someone. When giving feedback, you can
say:

> When you (the behavior), it causes (the result of the behav-
> ior—e.g., team results, personal issues, etc.), and makes me
> feel (feelings). Remenber to talk about specific behavoirs *not*
> attitudes or personalities.

This is less likely to cause defensiveness or blaming than
other approaches.

Tip 48. Follow the process for managing performance. Is
individual performance managed by the team or management
at your company? If it is managed by the team, is there a
process in place for reviewing individual performance? If not,
you could suggest a peer review panel of randomly assigned
coworkers who would review performance problems. You
might begin by looking at the process used to assign tasks: Was
this person assigned a workload comparable to other team
member's? Do team members volunteer for tasks? Is the workload unbalanced because some people see what needs to be
done, and others don't see those things? Are shortcuts being
taken, and if so, is the result less than the acceptable standard?
Are people just not held accountable for results? If individual
performance is managed by management, ask yourself
whether they are aware of the situation. If they are not, you
may want to discuss your feelings with your team leader. If
management is aware of the situation, and chooses not to deal

with it, your best choice may be to accept the situation as one which is outside your ability to change.

See Resource 17: Managing Team Performance

Tip 49. Make him feel like a full team member. If he seems not to care about the team, he may be feeling isolated. Restate the purpose and vision of the team to accomplish more together than each could accomplish on their own. Go out of your way to help him feel a stronger part of the team. You may not "feel" like making sure he shares a part of the glory when milestones are met, but be sure he gets to "taste" the rewards of individual and team accomplishments, as an incentive to future dedication. He may respond to "feeling included." Your feelings will follow your actions—act this way even if the feelings aren't there yet, and hopefully you will be rewarded by his response.

Tip 50. Try to be understanding if the person has personal or health reasons which may be contributing to a lessened energy level. Your caring may encourage them to contribute more. Think of how you would like to be treated if you were experiencing a personal or health problem.

Tip 51. Move them from your team as a last resort. It may be possible that after everything you do, some people simply won't fit well into your team. After giving them every opportunity to clearly understand what is expected of them and the consequences of not meeting those expectations, you may need to transfer them to another team or to terminate them. This may be outside your boundary conditions and needs to be cleared with the appropriate people (normally Human Resources, team leader, and senior management) even if it is part of your team's responsibilities. Only transfer people who have a good chance of fitting in better with another team, never knowingly pass along a performance problem to someone else. For some team members the only answer is to let them go. This will be a rare occurrence. Before you recommend termination to management, be certain that you have given your teammate a fair chance to perform. Conduct the termination in a humane and sensitive way, consistent with what ever laws, contracts, or other guidelines you use for these situations in your organization.

Category: Team Member Problems
Problem: Hurt Feelings

Tip 52. Begin by looking for a pattern. Is it usually the same person whose feelings are hurt? Is it usually the same source? Are the feelings justified (would most people be hurt if the situation happened to them)? What would you change if you could? You may find, for example, that the problem will be reduced if certain team members learn how to be more tactful, or if the team learns to be more sensitive to people who come from different cultures. Training classes in effective feedback or in multicultural awareness can help these kinds of situations. Check with your training coordinator to see if something can be made available.

Tip 53. Decide whether it is appropriate to resolve the problem as a team, or between individual team members. Some of the ideas in Resource 9: Facilitating Groups can be applied. It is the responsibility of all team members to identify and correct undesirable behaviors that lead to hurt feelings. Remember that hurt feelings are usually caused by misunderstandings. Open communication will alleviate many problems.
You might say:

> Hideo, I'm afraid that I or other teammates may have hurt your feelings. I'd like to understand what I did, so that I can avoid doing it again in the future. You're an important part of this team, and I don't want to be responsible for causing problems with you or our team.

See Resource 9: Facilitating Groups

Tip 54. Try to ignore the undesirable behaviors for a while and reward desirable ones (reinforce the opposite of what you want to eliminate). See if this may help to either modify the behavior causing hurt feelings, or help the people to not feel hurt by what others do.

Tip 55. Modify your operating guidelines to include something like "We will treat each other with dignity and respect." Then when the hurtful behaviors occur again, anyone on the team can point out that your team isn't living up to your agreements. See Resource 2: Using Principles, Guidelines, and Boundaries.

See Resource 2: Using Principles, Guidelines, and Boundaries

Tip 56. Ask for help from your team leader. Often the team leader has responsibility for issues like contribution to team goals and performance. If hurt feelings lead a team member to act in ways that affect morale or team performance, the leader may need to deal with the situation.

Category: Individual Team Problems
Problem: Personality Conflicts

Tip 57. Manage conflict effectively. Conflict plays an important role with teams. If conflict is managed effectively, the struggle can be a source of strength and creativity. Remember that the enemy is the conflict and not the people involved. The first step is to acknowledge that conflict exists. Assess your own perception of the situation. If the conflict is between you and one other person, approach the other person one-on-one without involving the team. Give feedback on their behavior, not on their attitude. Be specific. For example you might say:

> Klaus, I feel like we are butting heads a lot. In our last project meeting, for example, we disagreed on nearly every product parameter for the new generation of software we are introducing. Healthy disagreement is good, and I know it usually helps us come up with better ideas, but I think I may be letting this thing go too far. I realized the other day that I argue with you just to argue with you. I have heard from the other engineers that this is starting to slow down the work of the whole product introduction team. I think most of our disagreements can be worked out prior to the product review meetings if we will take the time to talk. We can either let this thing continue, or we can try to work it out. Do you want to give it a try? I'll buy you lunch.

Tip 58. If several team members are experiencing conflict with one person, it is the responsibility of each team member to give that person feedback. If this does not resolve the situation bring it to the attention of the team leader. Together they should decide how to best approach the individual involved. You may need to bring up the problem in a team meeting. Once approached, the individual then shares the responsibility of resolving the situation. To ensure this, make sure that you find some common ground. For example, all parties generally want to see the team successful, even if they don't want to change their behavior to suit one or two individual team members. If you can show how the behavior is affecting team performance (not just personal whims or preferences) you have a much better chance of successful resolution.

See Resource 8: Giving and Receiving Feedback

Tip 59.   Use a neutral third party to help mediate the problems. You may invite a representative from Human Resources, or someone else respected by both people. The third party will help the people:

- Identify how they will both benefit if the issue is resolved, and how they will lose if it is not.
- Demonstrate that they understand the other person's side of the situation by having them state the other person's point of view. The process isn't over until both parties can state the other person's side of the conflict to the satisfaction of that person.
- Develop a "get-well plan" that has specific steps both parties agree to do to resolve the situation.

Tip 60.   Sometimes disagreements can't be resolved and you should just acknowledge that there are differences and move on.

See Resource 15: Managing Team Conflict

Category: Individual Team Problems
Problem: Bullies

Tip 61.   Identify the unacceptable behavior and ask the person to change. Dysfunctional behaviors include such things as: being too aggressive (putting down other team members, lashing out, blaming, arguing unnecessarily), blocking (disagreeing without apparent reason, distracting with irrelevant issues), recognition-seeking (bragging), and dominating (controlling the team's discussion and decision-making process, claiming expertise). It is the responsibility of all team members to identify and correct dysfunctional behaviors. Identify the behavior, decide whether to address it as a team or one-on-one, describe the behavior that has been observed without attacking those involved, explain how it is disruptive to the team's progress, and get a commitment from those involved to change the behavior in the future.

See Resource 9: Facilitating Groups

Tip 62. When giving feedback, avoid blaming people. Having someone get defensive will only make the problem more difficult to resolve. You might use a statement such as:

> When you (the behavior), it causes (the result of the behavior—e.g., team results, personal issues, etc.), and makes me feel (feelings).

Tip 63. Team members need clear roles. Does this team member understand what is expected? If it's a team issue, have the team review and update the team charter. If it's a personal issue, identify common risks and benefits (how both parties will benefit if the issue is resolved, and how both parties stand to lose it if is not), and establish a common process for resolving this issue.

Tip 64. Try to understand why this person might be using bullying techniques. Is the team offering him an opportunity to be heard, and giving due consideration to his suggestions? Is an opposing suggestion too threatening to him? Is the team deferring to the team leader's wishes or someone else's wishes? Fixing the root cause may eliminate the undesirable behavior.

See Resource 10: Team Problem Solving

Tip 65. If the inappropriate behavior continues, and you are unable to bring about the needed change through individual or team conversations, you may want to consider forming a Team Performance Board. Charter four to six members of the team to act as a review committee for performance issues on the team. It should include a formal process, well documented and followed, with much help from the Human Resources department to ensure legality and process integrity.

See Resource 14: Building a Collaborative Team Environment
See Resource 15: Managing Team Conflict

Category: Individual Team Problems
Problem: Personal Problems

Tip 66. When people go through a very painful experience at home, it may be more difficult for them to give their full attention and energy to their work and their work relationships. In many ways, since we spend such a high proportion of our weekly hours in the workplace, our coworkers become a substitute family. Can you imagine how much it would mean to you if you were going through a painful experience and found your coworkers empathetic and supportive to you? If the situation is a temporary one, after which one might expect a period of healing followed by a return of full attention and energy to the work, team members should do everything possible to be a part of the healing process for this person. However, if his needs are so great that they cannot be balanced with the needs of the business (for instance, his need to talk about the problems means that other team members can't get their work done), help him investigate other alternatives such as employee assistance programs or private counseling.

Tip 67. Talk to people who bring problems from home. Perhaps you have a teammate who brings personal problems to the workplace on an ongoing basis. If it is making it difficult for one or more team members to accomplish their work, it needs to be addressed either individually or as a team. First, address it personally with them. You might say:

> Chong, it seems that each morning when we begin our shift, you have many things to tell me about what has happened the previous evening between you and your son. While I am very sympathetic to your situation and agree it must be very difficult to live with, I do not feel I can continue to give up 20 to 30 minutes each day. To meet the team goals and my personal goals, I feel I need to give my full attention to the work when my shift begins. This situation leaves me feeling sad, because I know you need someone to talk to. I wonder if we could look into some alternatives. Maybe we could talk over lunch.

Tip 68. If the behavior is affecting many members of the team, it could be addressed jointly by those people. Some of the ideas in "Dealing with Dysfunctional Behavior" in Resource 9: Facilitating Groups can be applied. It is the responsibility of all team members to identify and correct undesirable behaviors.

See Resource 9: Facilitating Groups

Tip 69. Be supportive, but don't give advice unless she asks for it. It can be very frustrating to observe someone you care about live her life in a painful or hurtful way. Sometimes an outsider has a keener sense of the dangers involved in such a lifestyle than the person in the situation is willing to admit. If your coworker only wants to talk about the situation, but is not asking for advice or help, do nothing more than listen, unless it's interfering with your own ability to get your work done. If the person is asking for advice or help, use "I" messages (instead of "you should") and try to "attract" her to results you have experienced or seen following certain choices. You might try to refer her to any number of resources available through work or the community. For your own peace of mind, remember that all adults get to make choices about how to live their own life. Accept that others have different values, and that (even if we feel sure we know a better way for them) it is their choice. Choices usually have consequences which follow. Accept that you cannot fix it for them until they want to fix it for themselves, and perhaps the peace you have in your own life will inspire others to want more peace in their own life. (Let go and let it be their problem, not yours.)

Tip 70. When giving feedback, avoid blaming or judging people. Believe that people are doing the very best they can with the knowledge and experience they possess at the moment.

See Resource 8: Giving and Receiving Feedback

Tip 71. If you think a coworker may be addicted to drugs or alcohol, you might consider attending support meetings—not to learn how to manipulate their life or behavior—but to learn how to set boundaries in your own life so you can live in peace, unaffected by their inappropriate behaviors.

Category: Individual Team Problems
Problem: Knowledge Hogs

Tip 72. Examine the reward systems. If individual team members are given recognition of any sort for personal achievement in competition with other team members (for instance, most units produced), there is no incentive for sharing helpful hints with other team members. Revisit your team charter and make certain everyone is fully committed to doing the work as a team, and that rewards encourage sharing the work and skills and techniques.

Tip 73.   Treat the problem not the symptom. Is there any dysfunctional behavior on the part of other team members which is contributing to this problem? For instance, was knowledge or assistance shared, but then a team member who had been helped was unappreciative? Perhaps the unwillingness to share skills or knowledge is only a symptom of another problem. Try asking the person who is not sharing the skills or knowledge what the reason is. You might say:

> Nong, you used to share ideas with the other members of the sales team all the time. But in the last three team meetings you haven't given a single idea. Have we done anything to make you uncomfortable expressing your suggestions?

Tip 74.   Decide whether it is an individual or team issue (is more than one person being affected by the behavior?). If it is affecting just one or two people, you might say:

> Wendy, I have noticed that you are able to assemble more widgets in an hour than the rest of us. If you would share your methods with me, I might become as productive as you are, and the team would stand a better chance to earn its bonus.

See Resource 14: Building a Collaborative Team Environment

   Category: Individual Team Problems
   Problem: Missing Commitments

Tip 75.   Review team member roles and responsibilities and, if appropriate, review and update the team charter.

See Resource 16: Team Member Roles and Responsibilities

Tip 76.   Avoid blaming people. Try to find and rectify the process that causes people to act in undesirable ways. Perhaps your team hasn't been effectively using good performance plans and meeting skills. Remember to clearly identify who will do what when you have made a team decision.

See Resource 6: Holding Effective Meetings
Resource 7: Goal Setting and Measuring Results
Resource 8: Giving and Receiving Feedback
Resource 12: Planning for Action
Resource 17: Managing Team Performance

Tip 77. If someone understands a task to be his responsibility, and isn't doing it, ask yourself how performance issues are handled at your company. Is the team empowered to deal with performance issues? If so, you might form a Team Performance Board. Charter the team (or some team members) to act as a review committee for performance issues. If the team is not empowered, you will need to appeal to management. If management is aware of the situation and chooses not to address it, accept that it is outside your sphere of influence and try your best to not let it bother you.

See Resource 16: Team Member Roles and Responsibilities

Tip 78. Use the "law of natural consequence." When a team member isn't performing there should be a natural consequence for his action. This could be disciplinary action as mentioned in the previous tips, or it might be something else. If a shipment is missed and a customer doesn't get their product on time, for example, the natural consequence might be an angry customer. If the team member is skilled in dealing with customers, have him be the person who must call and apologize to the customer. This firsthand experience with the natural consequence can be very educational.

Category: Individual Team Problems
Problem: Lack of Personal Accountability

Tip 79. Even in teams, each person is accountable for results. Review the team charter and make sure each person understands the division of tasks. This problem most commonly occurs when people think that someone else must be responsible for a certain activity. The team should have a clear process for deciding who does what. This is especially important because in most team-based organizations the same tasks are not always given to the same people. In traditional organizations, for example, all accounting work would be done by the accountant. In a team, however, some of this work might be done by other people periodically as decided by the team. The process might be a rotation schedule, a case-by-case team decision, or something as simple as a job jar that everybody draws a job from for their morning assignment.

Tip 80.   Tell the team member how his not accepting responsibility hurts the team. Use facts and figures. Refer to the process outlined in Resource 8: Giving and Receiving Feedback. Don't say "You're not a good team member," or "You're not pulling your fair share," be specific. Say:

> Joe, when you didn't complete your part of the report on time, the package to the customer was delayed by three days. As a result of the "no delay guaranteed" contract we have with them we lost 3 percent of our revenue on this project.

Resource 8: Giving and Receiving Feedback

Tip 81.   At a team meeting, develop a process together that is to be used if one member is not acting responsibly. Be sure all team members participate with suggestions.

See Resource 16: Team Member Roles and Responsibilities

Tip 82.   If someone understands a task to be their responsibility, and they aren't doing it, ask yourself how performance issues are handled at your company. Is the team empowered to deal with performance issues? If so, you might form a Team Performance Board. Charter the team (or some team members) to act as a review committee for performance issues. If the team is not empowered, you will need to appeal to management. If management is aware of the situation and chooses not to address it, accept that it is outside your sphere of influence and try your best to not let it bother you. Continue to offer encouragement and feedback whenever appropriate to this team member.

See Resource 16: Team Member Roles and Responsibilities

Category: Individual Team Problems
Problem: Breaking Old Habits

Tip 83.   Offer recognition and encouragement when others choose the new behavior over the old habit. Say:

Shaun, I know this cross-training idea has been hard for you, but when you just volunteered to teach the training class on safety, I felt like you were really being a member of the team. I appreciate that, and I'm looking forward to the class.

Tip 84. Practice a lot of patience, and believe that people are doing the very best they can. Sometimes we can only change a behavior for an hour or a day or a week. Provide a loving environment where they will be encouraged to practice the new behavior, until they win their own personal battle.

Tip 85. If you're having a problem taking your focus off a behavior, you may want to change one of your own habits as a way of having something else to think about. It will probably help you develop more empathy for their struggle!

Category: Individual Team Problems
Problem: Quiet Team Members

Tip 86. Ask him for an opinion at team meetings. If it isn't too embarrassing to him, you may need to say:

We've heard from almost everyone about this problem with the server. Mark, you have more experience on the computer than anyone, what do you think?

Tip 87. This person will probably respond best to affirmations and encouragement, to build trust that his ideas have worth. Many people are quiet because they fear public ridicule or failure. Likewise, very small doses of feedback or criticism will appear large to him. Try to appreciate the many diversities in personalities on the team, making sure to seek this shy person's opinions and input, but making an allowance for him to be the person he is.

Tip 88. Gradually, over time, see if this person is willing to accept leadership positions with the team to build self-confidence. Tasks with a known beginning and ending time would be an easy place to begin. For instance, could he research something and report back to the team? Or, could he agree to take notes at this meeting and read them back next time? Would he agree to be the one to collect the timecards each week this month? If your team does customer visits, could he go with someone this time, and then take a new teammate next time?

Three

Team Problems

Problems That Keep Teams from Being Effective

Category: Team Focus and Purpose
Problem: Unclear Roles

Tip 89. Clarify roles and responsibilities. When team members are not clear on their roles and responsibilities, even good teams may find themselves knocking heads and not getting the job done. The five basic steps to clarifying team member roles and responsibilities are:

- Analyzing the work to be done.
- Defining shared responsibilities.
- Defining individual responsibilities.
- Learning each other's roles.
- Reviewing roles and responsibilities on a regular basis.

Suggest the team work through the five steps together.

See Resource 16: Team Member Roles and Responsibilities for more information and a suggested process. Write down the roles and responsibilities for each member or put them on a matrix or chart and distribute them to each team member.

See Resource 16: Team Member Roles and Responsibilities

Tip 90. Clarify responsibilities when action planning. For each action item, write down who is going to do what by when. Check for understanding and acceptance of the responsibility by those accountable for the item. Be sure to document roles and responsibilities and post them and/or give a copy to each team member.

See Resource 14: Building a Collaborative Team Environment
Resource 16: Team Member Roles and Responsibilities

Tip 91. Figure out ways to help each other. As you learn what each other does on the team, look for ways to help. Ask each member on the team to answer this question:

What's one thing I need help on?

Then, see how many of those things can be done by helping each other. In doing so, you will learn who does what and improve the process at the same time.

Category: Team Focus and Purpose
Problem: Unclear Direction

Tip 92. Make plans. There are at least three basic plans every team needs to have:

1. A transition plan which shows how the overall organization is changing and how the team fits into it.
2. A results plan which the team uses to guide its efforts, prioritize resources and measure progress.
3. A team learning plan which outlines the education and experiences team members need to continuously improve.

Review each of these plans with the team and determine who should be doing what and by when. Write it down and give it to each team member. Repeat the process monthly or more frequently as needed.

See Resource 12: Planning for Action
Resource 17: Managing Team Performance

Tip 93. Review your charter, boundary conditions, and your team member roles and responsibilities matrix. Look for things that have yet to be done or are not being done often or well enough. Redistribute work if necessary. Identify and discuss roles and responsibilities until people are clear about what they are supposed to do, believe it can be done, and are committed to accomplishing it. If you haven't already established the charter, boundary conditions, and roles, go through a process to complete these for your team. Make sure to include the appropriate people in your process. Involve management, for example, in developing your charter to make sure that everyone has similar expectations of the team.

See Resource 1: Creating a Team Charter
Resource 2: Using Principles, Guidelines, and Boundaries
Resource 12: Planning for Action

Tip 94. Talk about the best use of your time. Sometimes some team members get done with their part of the effort first or have a slack period and they may not know what the work priorities are. Ask the question of the team:

> Based on all our plans and goals, what's the best use of this time right now?

Brainstorm a list and prioritize based on customer need and overall benefit to the organization. Get out of your box and be creative, perhaps the best use of their time is working outside the team altogether.

Category: Team Focus and Purpose
Problem: Confusion Between Team and Leaders

Tip 95. Involve your team leader in setting boundary conditions for your team to operate within. You might say:

> We're not clear exactly what we should be doing and how it fits with what you're doing. We believe it would help the team and you to have a way to talk about this and work on it together. Will you help us?

See Resource 2: Using Principles, Guidelines, and Boundaries
Resource 20: Being a Living Example

Tip 96. Clarify the team's responsibility versus the team leader's responsibilities at action planning time. Each time a team begins a new project, reorganizes, shifts individual responsibilities, or needs to get recommitted to its goals, the leader's role and the team roles may change. It's a natural part of the process. Set the expectation to renegotiate roles and boundaries frequently and review them often.

See Resource 16: Team Member Roles and Responsibilities
Resource 19: Team Leader Roles and Responsibilities

Tip 97. With the team and management participating, draw a map showing the work process as it progresses from step to step. Identify at each step:

- Who is to be involved in which decisions?
- Which member(s) of the team will decide what?
- What decisions the team leader will make?

Tip 98. Develop a transition plan identifying which responsibilities will be assumed by the team over what time frame. Keep it simple and graph it out if possible. Make it easy for management to take back responsibilities if things change on the team or if the task changes. It's best to assume that management wants the team to take on the responsibilities it can effectively handle and will let go when the time comes. It will put you in the right frame of mind to help them let go and take on new responsibilities of their own.

Category: Team Focus and Purpose
Problem: Unclear or Incorrect Boundaries

Tip 99. Clarify your boundaries. Sometimes boundaries are unclear. Perhaps they were clear when you started, but over time responsibilities and levels of authority shifted. Invite your team leader to a meeting to clarify your team's boundaries. Clearly state what areas are unclear and if possible describe the boundary conditions that you believe are appropriate for the team and the job it has to do now. It's important to have a true consensus on boundary conditions.

See Resource 3: Making Group Decisions

Tip 100. Make boundaries right. Sometimes boundary conditions are too loose or too tight. Conditions that are too loose usually paralyze the team by not providing enough structure for the team to operate in. Boundaries that are too tight are really management directives disguised as a set of boundaries. Both can be addressed in the same way. In conversation with your team leader, you might say:

> We feel the boundary conditions as they exist today aren't right for where we are as a team and we would like to renegotiate them with you. Will you meet with us so we can explain and adjust them appropriately? We want to get on with our work and get our job done.

At the meeting, be specific about the problem and how it keeps you from doing your job. Suggest a set of conditions that you believe would work better. Be ready to negotiate with an open mind.

Note: It's better to believe that management really does want your team to be successful and treat them that way in every meeting, especially about boundary conditions. It will put you in a better frame of mind and will help them learn to trust you.

Tip 101. Ask about changed boundaries. Sometimes boundary conditions are changed for no apparent reason. Few things make teams more angry than this. If the team gets mad, wait until you've calmed down. You might say to your team leader or whoever changed the boundaries:

> We're feeling unhappy about this change in boundaries. We know there must be a reason but we don't know what it is. Can you help us understand this situation better than we do now?

You might follow up by saying:

> How can we work with you in a way that we don't end up in this situation again? It really helps us to be involved if possible, or at least informed up-front about these types of things. Will you help us to do that?

Category: Team Focus and Purpose
Problem: No Team Guidelines

Tip 102. A quick way for a team to set guidelines or rules to manage itself by is to brainstorm a list of behaviors you would like to see in your team and a list of behaviors you wouldn't like to see in your team. Then, use those lists to develop a list of rules or operating guidelines. Work until the team can reach consensus on one list that the members promise to abide by.

See Resource 2: Using Principles, Guidelines, and Boundaries

Tip 103. When setting guidelines, don't dwell in the past. Look for positive ways to describe how you see the team acting when it is at its best. If people want to gripe about the past, you might say:

> Let's turn what we didn't like in the past to what we want to be in the future. We'll state the opposite of what we didn't like and make it something we want. Instead of saying, "she's always late," let's say as team members, "we keep our time commitments faithfully."

Tip 104. When working with guidelines, avoid using guidelines to blame other team members or use them to correct performance problems of individuals. Be a coach not a police officer. Guidelines should point toward positive behaviors.

If a person violates guidelines, remind them why it was put in place and how important it is for the good of the whole team. If they continue to violate the guidelines, see Resource 14: Building a Collaborative Team Environment.

See Resource 14: Building a Collaborative Team Environment

Category: Team Focus and Purpose
Problem: No Team Plan

Tip 105. Identify your key deliverables. Planning is a key part of almost every team's work. Without it you're as lost as a sailor without a chart or a star to steer by. At the very least you must agree on what the basic deliverables are for your team and who is going to do what to be sure they happen.

Tip 106. Get a plan. A simple five-step planning process includes:

1. Plan what action needs to be taken.

2. Plan who will do what.

3. Plan for necessary resources.

4. Take action.

5. Evaluate progress.

See Resource 12: Planning for Action

Tip 107. Identify needed resources. Teams often overlook or poorly plan resource requirements. Resource requirements can include the following:

- People—who will we need when?
- Time—how much will we need?
- Materials—what will we need?
- Budget—what monies will we need and when?
- Outside services—what outside help do we need?
- Equipment—what do we need?
- Support—what kind of management and practical help do we need?

Tip 108. Do results oriented planning. Results planning allows a team to pull it all together. It includes a performance plan specifying key result areas, a project plan with measurable goals and an action plan specifying what needs to be done and who will do it by when.

When developing a results plan, be specific about what must be done to meet your team's expectations. Do this by setting measurable goals and action plans for each key result area. Follow up with a learning plan which focuses on the skills and knowledge that must be attained to achieve the desired results.

See Resource 17: Managing Team Performance

Category: Team Focus and Purpose
Problem: Unclear Charter

Tip 109. Create a charter. Having a clear and shared sense of purpose is critical to a successful team start-up. Established teams who lose their sense of purpose are in trouble and will experience problems until they can get refocused. When creating a team charter, or modifying one you have, be sure to include the overall purpose of the team, your key customers, the key result areas, your guiding principles, and any time frames.

See Resource 1: Creating a Team Charter

Tip 110. Update your charter regularly. Charters go out of date rapidly. Updating them frequently helps remind the team why they are working together in the first place and focuses people's attention on a positive goal. It also allows you to modify your charter as the task or circumstances change. Be sure to involve your customers, suppliers, team leaders, and others from outside the team. Involving stakeholders makes it better for them and for you.

Tip 111. When preparing your team charter, prepare your own thoughts and ideas first. Really think about it for a day or more before you meet together. Then, jointly brainstorm all thoughts and ideas. From that develops a rough draft of the charter.

Remember, it's a rough draft, just get the key points down first. Allow the draft to incubate for a few days to give people a chance to really consider it. Then, finalize and distribute the charter. Don't let the process drag on. Strive for what works, not the perfect words.

See Resource 1: Creating a Team Charter
Resource 14: Building a Collaborative Team Environment

Category: Team Focus and Purpose
Problem: Lack of Follow-Through

Tip 112. If you find the team is constantly off plan, it may be that the plan is too specific for your changing environment. Try backing off on the detail of how things are going to be done, focusing instead on the deliverables of the team, the behaviors you expect from the team, even the attitude you need to be successful. In rapidly changing environments, a loose plan discussed very often, even daily for a few minutes, is often better than the traditional detailed product.

Tip 113. Sometimes being off plan continually is due to a poorly designed or executed planning process. Team planning and individual planning can go hand-in-hand, and most often should. Team planning includes creating a team charter, a team results plan, and a team learning plan. Individual planning includes a team member role description, individual results plan, and an individual learning plan. This sounds like a lot of work but it doesn't have to be very detailed to be effective. Once you learn how to do it, it doesn't have to take very long, either. It's well worth the up-front investment.

See Resource 17: Managing Team Performance

Tip 114. Being off plan continually can also be a team performance issue. Teams have performance problems just like individuals do. Sometimes they will commit to a plan or an outcome and then just ignore it.

It's better, however, to believe that more than 90 percent of the breakdowns that occur in teams are due to system and organizational problems, not a lack of commitment or laziness. It puts you in a more positive frame of mind to fix the problem rather than the symptom. Look for the system and organizational issues that drive people to ignore the plan before looking for individual performance problems.

See Resource 17: Managing Team Performance

Category: Team Focus and Purpose
Problem: Violating Guidelines

Tip 115. Determine why guidelines are violated. Guidelines are rules the whole team has agreed to for the good of the team and the customers the team serves. People who consistently violate the guidelines are hurting the team and should be shown how that behavior is holding the team back. If they persist, find out why. If it's a system problem, deal with it. If it's a lack of commitment or interest on the individual's part, then deal with that swiftly. Mature teams often address such issues openly, sharing their feelings and, if necessary, handing out sanctions as well. You might say to the individual:

> Bob, when you violate the rules we have all agreed to, it hurts us all. Last week you violated our rules on respecting others when you called Kathy a name, and you also violated our agreement to meet our commitments when you didn't finish the new actuarial tables on time. It makes it harder to do our jobs and we can't permit this to continue. We need your help. Can you help us understand why this behavior

persists? Also help us understand how it can be corrected. We need to find a way to fix this together. Will you work with us on this?

This will begin the process that the team should continue until the behavior changes, the guideline changes, or the person is asked to leave.

Tip 116. Perhaps it's time for the team to revise its guidelines. The reason they are not followed may be because they don't make sense anymore. Or, perhaps some of them never made sense but people followed them anyway for a while, then grew tired of them and began to do as they pleased. To revise existing guidelines, find out which ones seem to be working well, which ones don't seem helpful or important any more, what new problems or issues have emerged, and what new challenges face the team.

Guidelines are something the team must have a clear consensus about. The final version should be posted and a copy given to each team member.

Tip 117. Decide if this problem is the symptom or the cause. Ignoring guidelines you just helped to create is not the sign of a healthy or collaborative team environment. It may point toward deeper and more critical problems and potential misalignment of personal and team goals. Key elements of a collaborative team environment include a common purpose, trust, clear roles, open communication, diversity, and balance between the importance of completing tasks and building strong and healthy relationships between team members.

See Resource 14: Building a Collaborative Team Environment

Category: Team Performance
Problem: Unmet Goals

Tip 118. Clarify what the goals are, brainstorm specific actions to help achieve the goals and take appropriate actions to meet them. A process for clarifying goals is outlined in Resource 7: Goal Setting and Measuring Results. You could say:

Our goals are really important and we are not meeting them, let's devote our next meeting to finding ways to get on the road to successfully meet them.

See Resource 7: Goal Setting and Measuring Results

Tip 119. Assign several team members to regularly review progress toward meeting goals and have them present the progress at team meetings. One of the best ways to get back on track toward meeting goals is to make them a high priority by discussing them often.

Tip 120. Use visual displays that show how the team is performing. Charts that show poor performance will help the team focus on improving their results. Resource 10: Team Problem Solving and Resource 11: Tools for Problem Solving introduce a number of charting techniques a team may want to use.

See Resource 10: Team Problem Solving
Resource 11: Tools for Problem Solving

Tip 121. Ask yourself if you understand what the goal is and how best to achieve it. Chances are that if you don't understand it, other team members don't either. You might say:

> One of our ground rules says that there are no dumb questions. Well, I really don't understand our major performance goal. Is anyone else having the same problem?

If a team member can't help you understand the goal, find someone else in the organization who can explain it in a way you can understand.

Tip 122. Review the goals and your team's performance against them every team meeting. Make achievement of the goals the first and the last thing you think about every work day. Make them a regularly scheduled part of each team meeting or have a regularly schedule goal review at least monthly.

Tip 123. Use information you gathered with Resource 4: Building Customer Relationships to understand the implication of not meeting the goal.

> We developed this goal because of the information we received from our customers. If we don't meet the goal our customers are going to buy someone else's product.

See Resource 4: Building Customer Relationships

Category: Team Performance
Problem: Can't Say No

Tip 124. Determine if taking on too much responsibility is really the problem. This will prepare the team to discuss an appropriate solution with their team leader. Utilize a problem-solving technique outlined in Resource 11: Tools for Problem Solving. You might use the force-field analysis technique:

> We have been having trouble getting started on the ABC project. What are the forces for and what are the forces against our accomplishing the task?

After listing some forces for (e.g., budget, management support, good team members) and forces against (e.g., unclear responsibilities, multiple priorities, poor technology support, too many responsibilities) determine the relative strength of each listed item. You may find that another force is responsible for more of the project delay.

If having too much responsibility really is the problem discuss it with your team leader as soon as possible.

> We know the ABC project is important but after careful analysis have decided we cannot continue to be responsible for completing it. We need your help getting it reassigned or negotiating a new completion date.

See Resource 11: Tools for Problem Solving

Tip 125. Often teams can't handle responsibilities they have signed up for because team members need training in skills they do not have. Good problem solving may uncover this issue. If so, develop a plan to get the needed training using the process outlined in Resource 12: Planning for Action. Your team leader or training coordinator should be able to help you find internal and/or external resources to make sure the training happens and is of high quality.

See Resource 12: Planning for Action

Category: Team Performance
Problem: No Performance Feedback

Tip 126. Ask for feedback. It is important that team members manage their own need for information about their performance. Even the best intentioned teams cannot always know when individuals want performance feedback. Pay particular attention to the receiving feedback section of Resource 8: Giving and Receiving Feedback. Say:

> Sara, we've been working very closely on the new software installation. Would you mind giving me some feedback regarding my efforts?

See Resource 8: Giving and Receiving Feedback

Tip 127. Establish a performance feedback guideline. When team members understand and believe in their team's importance and purpose they will expect that all team members regularly discuss team and individual performance. If team guidelines do not explicitly point to the need for regular performance feedback look at the process for establishing guidelines outlined in Resource 2: Using Principles, Guidelines, and Boundaries.

See Resource 2: Using Principles, Guidelines, and Boundaries

Tip 128. Charter team members to develop a process for team performance feedback. Resource 17: Managing Team Performance details a methodology that helps teams assume responsibility for performance feedback from their team leader.

See Resource 17: Managing Team Performance

Category: Team Performance
Problem: Don't Know How to Improve

Tip 129. Ask other people and/or groups for improvement suggestions. Sometimes a fresh perspective is all it takes to help a team get over a barrier like this.

Tip 130. Ask your team leader for a new challenging/demanding performance goal. Exciting/difficult-to-achieve goals energize teams and help them find the energy to exceed their own expectations even when they have previously had difficulty figuring out how to improve.

Divide the performance goal into achievable segments using the tools provided in Resource 7: Goal Setting and Measuring Results and Resource 12: Planning for Action.

See Resource 7: Goal Setting and Measuring Results
Resource 12: Planning for Action

Tip 131. Talk to your customers about their expectations. They can often give you exciting ideas and help you refocus your energy on the things that are most important.

See Resource 4: Building Customer Relationships

Tip 132. Review your charter and plans. Have you accomplished them all? If so, create new ones by using input from stakeholders like corporate staff, customers, and vendors. If not, brainstorm ideas on how to accomplish your vision for your team.

See Resource 1: Creating a Team Charter
Resource 12: Planning for Action

Category: Team Performance
Problem: Stuck in Traditional Thinking

Tip 133. Place easels with opportunity statements written on them throughout the team's work area. When a team member has an innovative suggestion for handling the opportunity or problem they should write it on the easel. This will trigger other innovative ideas from the rest of the team and, possibly, other people who see the easels. An opportunity statement might say:

An opportunity ... the ABC process must be improved.

Occasionally seeing this statement will help team members keep the opportunity in mind and challenge them to think of new ways to deal with it.

Tip 134. Constantly look for new ideas from other companies. Do not get caught in the "not invented here" trap. Resource 4: Building Customer Relationships and Resource 5: Working with Suppliers each outline a process aimed at getting data about other companies. Adapt these processes to help your team get information about new ideas from other companies.

See Resource 4: Building Customer Relationships
Resource 5: Working with Suppliers

Tip 135. Always challenge team members when they assert that things cannot be changed or when they say things like, "We've always done it this way and we always will." Team success depends on constantly considering and implementing new ideas. Consider developing a team guideline that requires team members to constantly challenge old ways of thinking. The process is outlined in Resource 2: Using Principles, Guidelines, and Boundaries. The guideline might look like this:

> Our team is committed to challenging the way we do everything. It is required that all of us challenge each other when we think we are getting stuck in our old thinking patterns.

See Resource 2: Using Principles, Guidelines, and Boundaries

Category: Skills and Training
Problem: Lack of Work Skills

Tip 136. Have the team meet and brainstorm a list of all the technical and people skills that are required to perform all the jobs represented on the team. Often team members are not aware of all the skills required for success in a job. Develop a plan for obtaining the necessary skills. Resource 16: Team Member Roles and Responsibilities outlines a process that will result in a list of skills and a plan for cross-training team members in all of them.

See Resource 16: Team Member Roles and Responsibilities

Tip 137. Make acquisition and improvement of skills an ongoing process. Team members will learn and retain more information if they see training as a critical part of their job rather than an event.

Create a matrix with all the critical skills across the top and the names of all the team members down the left side. Then, with the input of team members and the approval of the entire team, assign dates for when team members will get training and coaching in all the skill areas where they need it.

Tip 138. Consider whether training requests are based on skill deficiencies (people do not know how to accomplish a certain task) or on will deficiencies (people do not want to accomplish certain tasks) before you decide to invest time and money in training. The following actions will help you make this decision:

- Always remind teammates during team meetings that training is expensive in terms of time and money. Then ask them to consider why they are asking for training. Is it because they do not want to do the task or because they truly need training?

- Often teammates will avoid unpleasant tasks by asking for more training. For example, interpersonal conflict is easy to avoid. The reason is often that people don't want to confront others rather than that they don't know how to confront others. The acid test is this: If your life depended on doing something (like confronting someone), could you do what is being asked for? If you couldn't do it and do it well, it is a *skill* problem that requires training. If you could do it but don't, it is a *will* problem. Will problems usually require changing organizational systems such as the way people are rewarded.

Tip 139. Often the best place to find training resources is within your own team. When a request is made for training, first try to find someone on your team and ask him to take time to provide coaching for the person who requested the training.

Tip 140. Create a list that includes all team members who have provided training and the specific training they provided. Post this list where everyone can see it so they can easily identify a training resource when they need it.

Category: Skills and Training
Problem: Lack of Technical Skills

Tip 141. Develop a technical skill buddy system. Assign each team member to be the buddy of another team member. Base the assignments on technical strengths and weaknesses. If a team member is strong in skills A, B, and C and weak in skills X, Y, and Z find another team member who is strong in X, Y, and Z and weak in A, B, and C.

Tip 142. When qualifying equipment vendors make sure they have high-quality training programs. Use these programs as the basis for your technical training program. Resource 5: Working with Suppliers and Resource 4: Building Customer Relationships outlines a process for developing relationships with suppliers. Make sure that the kind of training they can provide is an important criterion you use when selecting suppliers for ongoing relationships.

See Resource 4: Building Customer Relationships
Resource 5: Working with Suppliers

Tip 143. Consider training resources available at community colleges or training vendors. Many of these organizations have excellent vocational and interpersonal skills programs. In some cases they may be willing to develop programs to meet your needs if they address a wide enough audience (e.g., soldering skills, conflict resolution, etc.).

Category: Skills and Training
Problem: Lack of People Skills

Tip 144. Many people-skills problems occur because team members are not aware of and/or have not practiced the basic communication skills of effectively getting a message across and listening. Resource 13: Team Communication Basics outlines these skills and provides a framework for evaluation of the way your team communicates. When you observe a communication issue on your team you might say:

> I think we all need to spend time refining our communication skills. I know I can use some practice with my listening skills. Let's schedule time at our next meeting to review skills for effectively communicating a message across and doing a better job of listening.

See Resource 13: Team Communication Basics

Tip 145. Often training alone is not the answer to solving people problems. Some teams report that certain problems don't change after people-skills training sessions. Consider the following ideas if you are hearing this concern:

- Attending people-skills training is simple, but using the training on the job is difficult. Some people view these skills as corny or unnecessary. Others view them as too difficult or awkward. Teams need to continually challenge themselves to use the skills they learn in people-skills training sessions and then hold all members accountable for using the skills.

- The people-skills problem may be a symptom of another problem. A good place to look for the root of the problem is outlined in Resource 14: Building a Collaborative Team Environment. Successful teams have a common purpose, high levels of trust, clear roles, open communication, diversity, and a balance of task and relationship. If any of these are missing or are not fully considered you may be on your way to identifying the root of the people-skill problem.

See Resource 14: Building a Collaborative Team Environment

Tip 146. Ask your team leader to provide coaching and assistance as you work to use the training you have received. You might approach your team leader and say:

> I really enjoyed the listening skills training but I know it is going to be difficult for me to get in the habit of listening more effectively. Would you mind meeting with me after our next team meeting to give me feedback on how well I listened during the meeting?

Tip 147. Develop a learning and resource library for people to use for personal and team skill development. Collect books, guides, tapes, software, and samples of training materials for people to use as references. Preview materials from training vendors that can be ordered for just-in-time delivery to your team.

Category: Skills and Training
Problem: Resistance to Cross-Training and Rotation

Tip 148. Make an appropriate level of cross-training a requirement. Success for many teams requires rotation and cross-training. In an ideal team world everyone will want to take part. In reality some team members will drag their feet and resist becoming involved in the rotation and cross-training program. If rotation and cross-training are critical to your team's success it may be necessary to make participation a performance requirement. The team leader could say:

> Our long-term success depends on rotation and cross-training. I expect that all team members will become involved in this program as a performance requirement.

Tip 149.   Determine what is needed for your team. Some jobs do not lend themselves to rotation or cross-training. Often resistance to rotation occurs because the people in these jobs know this to be the case. Team leaders and team members should consider the following when they are determining if a job should be part of a rotation program:

- Do the technical requirements of the position create such a steep learning curve that it will take too long to transfer the knowledge/skills for an employee to be successful?

- Are the technical requirements based on a degree program requiring classroom as opposed to on-the-job training?

If the answer is "yes" the position may not be part of the regular cross-training program.

Many resisting employees will have great cases for why their position should not be part of the cross-training program. Teams must be very critical about which positions are exempted from the rotation and cross-training program. If it is too easy for a position to be exempted you will harm the long-term success of the program.

Tip 150.   Rotation and cross-training programs are good prospects for skill-based pay systems. Work with your Human Resources department to develop a skill-based pay system where employees have the ability to make more money as they learn more skills. This may help to overcome the initial resistance employees often feel when rotation programs are put into place. Keep the following issues in mind:

- Do not create a skill-based pay system as the way to lead people into teams. Employees will focus on the pay system rather than on the development of the team.

- Create your team and allow it to function for a period of time prior to initiating a skill-based pay system. This will allow you to identify the right skills for the program.

- Changes to pay systems take a long time. Be persistent and patient about the changes you would like to make.

Category: Skills and Training
Problem: Distributing Bad Jobs

Tip 151. Get rid of bad jobs. Having the same people always do the bad jobs creates tension and inequality in the team. If you cannot eliminate these jobs contract them out.

Tip 152. If bad jobs can't be taken out of the team rotate them. Create a job assignment rotation chart that is displayed where everyone on the team can see it. Include the names of all the team members and the jobs they are capable of performing. As appropriate, rotate job assignments based solely on which team members are capable of performing which jobs. This allows everyone a chance to do any of the jobs they are prepared for and helps them plan their personal learning goals for jobs they may not be currently trained to perform.

Tip 153. Tell your team if you feel you always get the bad jobs. Prepare for the discussion using Resource 15: Managing Team Conflict and Resource 13: Team Communication Basics. You might say:

> I feel as though I have been taking on all of the tough assignments for the past three weeks. I have been trained to do other tasks and would like to rotate into one of them next week.

See Resource 13: Team Communication Basics
Resource 15: Managing Team Conflict

Category: Skills and Training
Problem: Jack of All Trades, Master of None

Tip 154. Take cross-training very seriously. Cross-training allows team members to have empathy for each other and to operate more flexibly and effectively. But it must be done properly or it will create more problems than it solves. Do not allow team members to perform jobs they are not totally qualified for. Qualification should include both safety and technical proficiency requirements. Resource 16: Team Member Roles and Responsibilities provides a method to allow your team to understand who is qualified to perform which job. If you see a team member performing a job they are not qualified for, you might say:

> Alex, I know you have almost completed the training on the XYZ machine and are excited about taking on the responsibilities of this job but you should not operate it until Mary is available to help you complete your training.

See Resource 16: Team Member Roles and Responsibilities

Tip 155.   Create realistic expectations for how long it takes to learn a new skill and make sure team members support the time frame. When you prepare to train a team member you might say:

> Sally, I'm excited about training you in the ABC process. If you are available for two hours of training each week, it will take 12 weeks for you to become proficient with this process.

Tip 156.   Require team members to focus on the attainment of only one (two at the most) skill at a time. People will fully learn a skill more effectively when they focus their energies. Team members often sign up for as many training opportunities as possible with very good intentions of becoming proficient in all of them. Unfortunately, this often leads to a situation where they know a little bit about a lot things.

Tip 157.   Be certain about which skills should be crosstrained. In many teams there are certain skills that only a few technical experts can remain proficient in. If your team has positions like this, you might remove them from the normal rotation schedule.

Tip 158.   Remember that most work skills are best mastered by doing them for a sustained period of time. If your team has people who know several skills but who can't apply them well, consider changing the rotation or cross-training program to include a minimum time requirement for performing the task (from several weeks to a few years, depending on complexity) and a minimum application requirement at some regularity to keep current on the skills (so many days/weeks a year of doing critical tasks to maintain qualification status). Pilots, for example, must go through a rigorous training process to get a license to fly airplanes, but they must also fly a minimum number of hours every year to keep that license.

Category: Skills and Training
Problem: Skill Development

Tip 159. Recognize that people learn in different ways. About 60 percent of people learn best by doing the thing you are training them. The other 40 percent are evenly divided between learning by reading, learning by seeing, and learning by hearing. You should use all of these strategies (doing, reading, seeing, and hearing) as you train team members. You could even begin your first training session with a teammate by saying:

> I learn best when I hear someone explain a skill and then get a chance to practice on my own. How do you like to learn new tasks?

Tip 160. An important part of learning is having the opportunity to make mistakes, learn from them, and correct them the next time you try. Trainers need a great deal of patience. Often it is easier to jump in and correct the mistake rather than let the person you are training learn. Resist this temptation. Make it okay for the people you are training to make mistakes by saying:

> When I learned how to operate this software I always made mistakes. I want you to do the same thing. If you have a question please ask, but don't be afraid to try something and have it not work the first time. I'll be here to make sure you don't break anything.

Tip 161. Don't sign up to be a trainer if you do not fully understand the skill you are going to be training. Trainers who do not know their stuff create confusion rather than learning.

Tip 162. Have a skill development plan. This will help you know which skills people need to develop and will provide a schedule for your team's training. Remember to include different kinds of training in your plan. Classroom training, for example, should only be a portion of the activity. Training on working with customers might include classroom training, customer visits, and so on.

Category: Communication
Problem: Getting Your Case Heard

Tip 163.   People who do not have a high level of position or
status can use a combination of three strategies for getting
their ideas heard. First, clearly define the idea. This includes
providing a well thought out description of what the team will
gain by implementing the idea; how it fits the company's
strategy; the cost trade-offs; and potential risks and benefits.
Second, identify whose support will be needed to get the idea
implemented. If this is your team, get on the agenda of a future
meeting. Finally, do not give up if the idea is initially ignored,
sidestepped or altered. Listen carefully to the feedback and see
how it can be used to help you improve your idea. Be assertive
in your attempts to get the idea heard.

Tip 164.   Present ideas the right way. Sometimes the manner in which an idea is presented affects the likelihood that it
will be implemented by the team. When presenting an improvement idea avoid placing blame on someone or some team
for past mistakes or failures. Keep focused on known facts by
stating what the idea is and how you believe it will address the
issue or opportunity the team faces. For example, say:

> I have an idea I'd like us to consider that will save about an
> hour a week in paperwork. Would you like to hear it?

Rather than:

> I don't like all the paperwork we do. What idiot came up
> with these forms anyway?

Tip 165.   If an improvement idea is particularly controver-
sial or likely to have strong opposition among several members
of the team, it is helpful to discuss it with them prior to
presenting it at a team meeting. Listen very carefully to the
concerns and the ideas that are voiced by using the techniques
outlined in Resource 8: Giving and Receiving Feedback. Get a
feel for what will be required to gain their support and commitment. Determine if you can incorporate any of their suggestions into your proposal. People will usually support ideas they
participate in developing.

See Resource 8: Giving and Receiving Feedback

Category: Communication
Problem: Poor Communication

Tip 166. The source of poor communication can be with the sender of the communication, the receiver of the communication, or a combination of both the sender and receiver. (Typically, both the sender and receiver are not utilizing effective communication skills if there is an ongoing problem.) Try to identify the source of the poor communication and review with them good communication skills as they are described in Resource 13: Team Communication Basics.

See Resource 13: Team Communication Basics

Tip 167. If a teammate is not communicating well with you (e.g., not listening, being judgmental in conversation, quickly dismissing your ideas), provide the teammate with feedback about her communication. Provide this feedback using effective feedback techniques by focusing on the specific behavior you have observed and the affect it is having on you.

Tip 168. Set in place an operating guideline that identifies the kind of communication and interactions among team members the team wants to have on an ongoing basis. Refer to these operating guidelines in times when communication within the team is not effective as a way to get it back on track.

Tip 169. When interacting with another individual, it is helpful to rephrase the key points made from his comments. This accomplishes two important outcomes:

- It checks your understanding of what has been said.
- It demonstrates to the other individual that you are actively listening to what she is saying.

Tip 170. Make sure that you have an adequate forum for communication to occur. Each team should have a regularly scheduled team meeting and a place to meet. Use good meeting skills like those described in Resource 6: Holding Effective Meetings.

See Resource 6: Holding Effective Meetings

Tip 171. Ask the right kinds of questions. The types of questions that are used during conversations or interviews can either help gain additional information or can actually serve to close-up interaction. When attempting to gain considerable information about an issue, it is useful to use open-ended questions. An example of an open-ended question would be: "What is it about our scheduling system you like? Dislike?"

An open-ended question will tend to elicit a response that may address why, how, what, when, and who. By contrast, a close-ended question will provide you with a "yes" or a "no" giving you information of limited value. For example: "Do you like our scheduling system?"

Category: Communication
Problem: Rumor Control

Tip 172. Confront rumors. Rumors can be destructive within a company and/or within a team. When hearing what you suspect is a rumor, focus on the known facts. Ask questions of the person who is telling you the rumor such as: "How do you know this to be true?" or "What evidence or factual information do you have?"

The goal is to stop untrue rumors from spreading throughout the organization where they can have a negative affect on morale by quickly getting down to the facts.

Tip 173. If rumors are a persistent problem, put in place a team operating guideline that asks team members to commit to discussing only facts and never rumors.

If rumors persist, confront the rumor spreaders. Say "You don't know that's true. I won't be a part of spreading rumors. Please stop."

Tip 174. If a destructive rumor about a specific individual is being spread do not pass it on.

Tip 175. If the rumor revolves around an issue that is highly pertinent to the team (e.g., an impending reorganization), identify the person within the company who can Resolve the rumor and have a team member call him directly or invite him to attend the next team meeting. Explain to this individual the rumor that has been circulating and that the team is asking for him to provide the facts in the matter so that the truth in the matter can be known. You might say:

Jack, we're having a problem that is getting in the way of us getting our work done. We heard a rumor that there was a reorganization being considered. Would you mind coming into our team meeting on Thursday and sharing the facts of the situation with us? Even if you don't know anything about it, it would be helpful for the team to hear that directly from you. We'd like to get this put to rest so we can focus our attention back on our customers where it should be.

Category: Communication
Problem: Violated Expectations

Tip 176. If a team member has violated a commitment he made to the team, it is important to first seek to understand why the commitment was missed. By first understanding, the tendency to want to punish the person is lessened. The team may even discover there are sound reasons why the commitment was not kept. The goal is to overcome the difficult position the missed commitment has put you in by taking positive actions, not to punish the person who missed the commitment.

Tip 177. If you have violated a team commitment, acknowledge it immediately to the team. State specifically what the commitment was you failed to keep, the impact you believe it has had on the team, and specific actions you will take to help improve/correct the situation. For example:

I wanted everybody to know that I didn't get my sales forecast done yesterday as promised. I know that it is holding up our marketing plan. I had a problem with my software and I have Jim helping me to get the compiler working properly right now. I'll have it done no later than 10:00 a.m. tomorrow morning.

Tip 178. Ask the team member what you can do to help. If necessary, move people off less important projects to get the plan back on track.

Category: Interpersonal Problems
Problem: Unresolved Issues

Tip 179. Have a clear process the team agrees to use for solving problems. Sometimes issues go unresolved simply because people don't know what to do when problems arise. Consider the following five-step process for your team:

1. Write a clear and concise statement of the problem.

2. Jointly agree on root causes (the reasons behind the symptoms).

3. Explore possible solutions to the root causes as you consider the problems from several different angles. Brainstorming, a process of generating a lot of ideas without evaluating them or discussing their merit until the process is complete, is one good way to encourage diverse and creative approaches.

4. Select a practical solution and course of action that everyone understands and can commit to.

5. As a group, create an implementation plan that includes what is to be done, who will do it, when each step needs to occur, and a list of the resources needed.

See Resource 10: Team Problem Solving

Tip 180.   Jump in and do something. Remember that anything that limits your ability to accomplish your charter is a problem. Sometimes the hardest part of solving a problem is just getting started. It is easier to avoid the situation than to be the first one to say that something is wrong. Don't avoid problems with the hope that they will go away. Most won't be resolved without some sort of an active problem-solving process. One way to get this process started is to review the affect of the problem on the team's ability to meet its charter. By discussing the elements of the charter, team members can recognize cause for concern and get specific about possible areas of improvement without blaming. You might say:

> I know that some of us have noticed that our team doesn't always see eye-to-eye with our facilities support organization. We need them to accomplish our charter. They make our customers feel valued and welcome when they visit. I think the time has come to talk about this issue to see how we all feel about it, and to decide if any action is appropriate.

Tip 181.   Make problem solving a normal part of work, not an infrequent event. Occasionally teams do not confront problems because it is difficult to acknowledge that everything is not going according to plan. Team members can be embarrassed and reluctant to identify a need for improvement. This becomes worse if problem-solving activities are rare, or if they occur only when there are monumental problems. Make this a regular part of your work week. Have it on your regular agenda for team meetings. Face the issues and ask for help from others. You may do this effectively by:

- Stating what the original target, goal, or objective was.
- Providing your team members with a brief outline of the situation, identifying areas of concern.
- Requesting their ideas and comments about how to resolve the problem.
- Developing a new action plan that will either correct the situation or outline who else you need to talk to in order to get the data or resources you need.

Category: Interpersonal Problems
Problem: Conflict and Confrontations

Tip 182. Recognize the signs of unresolved issues and do something about it. Conflicts are not being resolved when factions exist, when there is reason to believe that team members are often not authentic with each other, when "parking lot" or off-line conversations occur frequently rather than candid discussion in team meetings, and when team members react with levels of anger or emotion that seem out of proportion. When one or more of these symptoms is occurring, it is time to bring up the issue in a meeting, grit your teeth, and determine to deal with the conflict before it gets any worse. Candidly discuss why you think you haven't dealt with the issue up to this point, apologize, and get on with engaging the team in a process to seek a solution.

Tip 183. Start with a clear statement of the situation. It is surprising how several people can be involved in the same disagreement and come away with completely different views on what happened and what the issues were. Once agreement has been reached on the issue at hand, then those involved (or the entire team) must take responsibility for resolution.

Tip 184. Use a good conflict resolution process. It helps diffuse the emotion. Handling conflict and confrontation is uncomfortable for almost everybody. People usually go to great lengths to act as if conflicts don't exist, and we all tend to push disagreements, anger, and disruptive behavior under the rug. While it is almost impossible to make this situation painless and comfortable, there are conflict resolution tools available that can minimize the pain. If the conflict affects the whole team:

- Put the conflict in perspective within the overall purpose and goals of the team.
- Identify common risks and benefits.
- Establish a common process for resolving the conflict.
- Provide everyone an opportunity to voice their point of view on issues involving them.
- Ask questions to clarify needs and expectations.
- Focus on cause and effect—not just the effect.
- Maintain mutual respect and involvement.
- Work for what is best for the team.
- Write an improvement plan together.

It is this joint approach to responsibility, understanding, selecting solutions, and creating a plan that is the key to the success of this process.

See Resource 15: Managing Team Conflict

Tip 185.   Change your way of thinking about conflict. Confrontation has typically been associated with unpleasantness and anger, something to be avoided at all costs. Individuals who have been raised to avoid conflict and confrontation have often learned to "sweep under the rug" any ideas or attitudes that may lead to unpleasantness. While this delays having to manage the situation, the underlying conflict still remains, and will usually resurface at a later time. Eventually, the conflict and the anger that results will grow unchallenged, possibly to seriously damage the team by breaking it into factions or fostering disillusionment and discontent. The result of finding a way to not deal with conflict will be much more serious and may cause permanent damage to the business.

This way of thinking must be challenged and changed if we are ever to push ourselves to reach our potential. Conflict can be managed so that it is productive and not unpleasant. It is usually a struggle between two or more people who simply have differing ideas and expectations and very seldom is a battle between absolute right and wrong. Once we can get clarity about the usefulness of conflict in generating the very best ideas (often the product of both points of view), we can learn to use this valuable tool for the best interest of our team and business.

Category: Interpersonal Problems
Problem: Using Diversity

Tip 186. Create diversity (e.g., race, gender, culture, age, education, physical ability, job function, etc.) in your team. It is natural that we are most comfortable around people who are like us—they validate our point of view. We know how to act and what to expect, and we usually don't offend people. So it is natural that we create teams with the same type of people on them. But teams that are composed of people with the same background are usually not effective over time. They look at problems the same way and usually come up with the same ideas over and over again. Diversity creates fresh perspectives and fosters creativity and innovation in a team. But this requires that we respect people who are different from us.

Tip 187. Respect ideas that are different from yours. One productive and creative way to react to diversity is to make a personal commitment to not judge new ideas immediately, but to make a concerted effort to understand and build on those ideas. It has been shown that we, as individuals, can make a conscious decision to hold back from immediately evaluating ideas, and can change our own responses to new concepts. By being diligent in this area, you will not only be more open and receptive to new thoughts and perspectives, you will also be a wonderful example to other members of the team.

Tip 188. Do some diversity awareness raising activities. Sometimes appreciating diversity is difficult because individuals have never experienced different backgrounds, traditions, values, and approaches before. For example, if you have never been close friends with someone of another faith or cultural background, their traditions and expressions and everyday ways of life will be very difficult to understand.

The team leader can bring in an individual to talk to the team about other cultures, languages, and religions, and the beliefs and biases that are found in them. This speaker can help to bring alive the total picture, and the ways in which those traditions were developed long ago. This speaker can help everyone to understand the diversity the members of the team represent, and the richness found within that diversity. Finally, the team can learn that there really are very few "right and wrong" kind of situations, and that, through diversity, we each bring an area of strength to the team. There are also excellent training activities available to help people understand other aspects of diversity, including our own unintentional biases. See your training coordinator or Human Resources representative for more information.

Tip 189. Confront diversity problems immediately. Even though allowing an occasional comment may seem like the best approach (we don't want to make a mountain out of a molehill), any tolerance of closed thinking will send a strong signal to the team that it is acceptable to shut out others based on bias and prejudice. It is never inappropriate to speak out in support of new and different ideas or to confront subtle biases. Race, gender, age, religious, or cultural jokes are never appropriate in a team setting even when they have nothing to do with anyone on the team. In confronting these biases you might say something like:

> Simon, I know your comment about Dana not working on her Sabbath was not intended to hurt her, but I think it's important that we recognize that her religious commitments are as important to her as yours are to you. We owe it to each other to respect each other's cultures and values, and we should realize that this is what makes our team strong and successful.

Tip 190. Create common ground. Have diversity in team composition but share common team values as a way to resolve conflicts and focus on the same overall goals. Each team member must be able to support and commit to the values of the business and the team, as these are the fundamentals behind all the decisions and actions that occur throughout the course of running the business. An example of team values are those we use at BFR:

- Do what is right.
- Do what helps others.
- Do it together.
- Do what makes sense.

These words, and the words we use to explain and discuss them, are the very fabric of our team. They bind us together through every situation we encounter. Your team should support your own team values as well. Charters, operating guidelines, goals, and boundary conditions mentioned elsewhere in this guide are also useful things to help your team have common grounding and focus as a way to channel and direct your creativity.

Category: Interpersonal Problems
Problem: Handling Mistakes

Tip 191. Make it okay to make mistakes. Most people who've worked in organizations for a while come to accept as truth that it is wrong to make mistakes. They may hesitate to try new tasks, suggest a new idea, or offer an opinion when they're not sure of the outcome of doing something risky. While this kind of behavior makes us all feel safe and comfortable, it in fact has a negative effect on the long-term health of the business. It results in decisions being made without all the pros and cons on the table, suggestions for better processes never coming up, and new ideas being agreed to based on who supports them rather than their merit.

The team can (and should) make every effort to change this kind of thinking. Here are some suggestions for team members faced with this situation:

- Plan to initiate a discussion in a team meeting about this topic. Cite some recent examples of times when others have held back potentially helpful ideas or not stated their true feelings (using yourself in the examples is a good idea) as decisions are made. Discuss how this ultimately effects the performance of the team.

- Make an agreement among yourselves to change your own attitudes so that making mistakes is seen as not only acceptable, but a critical part of the learning process for the team. Add this agreement to your guidelines.

- Discuss what reactions and consequences typically occur when mistakes are made now. Then define how you'll react to mistakes in the future.

- Acknowledge that changing perceptions is difficult and takes time. Recognize that you'll often need to remind and reinforce each other.

Tip 192. Team leaders should set the proper example. Sometimes when team members are afraid to make mistakes, there are valid reasons for those feelings. Perhaps the manager or team leader has always taken a dim view of those who make mistakes. Maybe those who made mistakes were held up as negative examples in team meetings, or were not given opportunities to try new things until they "corrected the problem." And probably, the team leader is just as hard on herself when she happens to make a mistake. All this leads to hiding mistakes (and certainly not discussing them openly), and encourages a workplace where blaming is common.

The team leader can very effectively help to correct this situation. By being a "living example," she can begin to not just talk about how it should be but actually show through her actions that there is no disgrace in making mistakes and that we can all learn from them. She can do this by

- Talking about her own mistakes openly and without embarrassment with the whole group.

- Responding pleasantly and without negative emotion when a mistake occurs.

- Remind the people involved that there is no assumption that mistakes get made because people are stupid, lazy, or don't care about the team.

- Continuing to provide a broad business perspective so that the individual incident is not blown out of proportion.

- Helping with planning for correction so that team members have an ally in creating the solution.

See Resource 20: Being a Living Example

Tip 193. Provide coaching and information resources to help avoid unnecessary mistakes and to react appropriately when there are mistakes. Business information provides the broadest possible context for the team, and coaching gives team members someone to talk with candidly as they review options and develop action plans. When faced with a situation where a team needs support in handling a difficult situation, the team leader might say:

> Let's look at the elements of this situation. Our sales team has decided that we could really benefit from weekly, instead of monthly, reports on products shipped. I think you folks have done an excellent job reviewing your needs and outlining how this change would benefit us all. I also think you've done a fine job of maintaining an open and helpful relationship with our finance group. I suggest we set up a meeting for our team and theirs, and send them the agenda in advance so they can have input to it. We should be sure that we also review their needs, and get their ideas on solving this dilemma.

Tip 194. Use just-in-time training. It is normal and natural that teams make mistakes. Sometimes this calls attention to a need for more information. Sometimes this identifies a need for training, where teams spend time learning new skills and acquiring new tools.

Just-in-time learning has been shown to be exceptionally effective in these situations where the team needs to respond quickly to a mistake. This means that as soon as an area of need is identified, then appropriate training is found and used to help the team. (This is different from situations where lots of training is scheduled as part of a normal educational curriculum and team members are required to recall the needed information and skills later when they're needed back on the job.)

To provide training to team members, first look at the areas where more skills, experience, or knowledge are needed. Second, find the most appropriate training program for your team (something practical, affordable, easy to use, and directed at your specific need). Finally, schedule the training so it doesn't disrupt other team activities and can be applied quickly to help your situation.

Tip 195. Reinforce proper mistake management. Some suggestions you might want to consider to provide positive reinforcement to the team as team members risk making mistakes include:

- Having an agenda item at a regular meeting to review mistakes that have been made and what the people involved can share with others from these experiences.

- Asking the team leader to review her own mistakes and to volunteer what was learned.

- Scheduling a time at your team leader's staff meeting with her boss to present our business reasons for allowing an occasional mistake because it provides learning and encourages disagreements that ultimately result in the best solutions for the business.

- Presenting an award to team members whose resolution of mistakes created the most learning for the team.

Category: Interpersonal Problems
Problem: Hygiene Problems

Tip 196. Be sensitive to the person's situation. Instances where someone on the team has a hygiene problem are extremely rare. However, when they do occur, they are probably the most difficult issues for anyone to deal with. We are all uncomfortable to some degree about the idea of mentioning our concerns with someone's hygiene. While avoiding the issue by not acknowledging the problem allows us to not hurt anyone else's feelings, we instead allow a larger issue to remain that may disrupt the team. Any time a situation results in one individual being avoided, talked about, or ridiculed, it becomes a business issue and positive action is called for. Some guidelines for dealing with the situation follow.

- Remember it's understandable that you're embarrassed by the situation, and are uncomfortable talking about anyone else's personal issues.

- We must also remember that we are unqualified to make assumptions about why this issue (or any hygiene issue) exists. For example, bad breath may seem to result from poor dental hygiene, but could also result from an abscessed tooth, a digestive problem, prescription medication, or a nontraditional diet.

- Mentioning the situation from a sense of concern and regard for the individual is important.

- Remembering to put the situation into a business context.

Tip 197. Be clear and discreet. Once an issue with an individual's hygiene has come up, discretion is of the utmost importance. There are a few basic steps to help in handling the situation that put responsibility on the shoulders of the right people and maintain privacy.

- State clearly what you've noticed and why you're concerned, without any reference to causes.

- Reinforce how important this individual is to the group, and why that led you to believe that a candid approach was the only honest and caring thing to do.

- Reassure that the entire situation is not only private, but also that the next steps are up to the person.

- Remind the person of any resources available to him or her, like a company nurse, that might be a confidential and affordable alternative.

- Show that the relationship between the individual and yourself is based on much more than this small problem, and be diligent in discussing other business issues and not dwelling on it. You could say:

> Margaret, I need to bring up something that seems to have recently been affecting your interaction with customers and team members, and I am pretty uncomfortable doing this. I have noticed that you have bad breath, and I'd like to do everything I can to help you to take care of this problem. You're a real important member of our team, and we need you now as much as we ever have. I'd be happy to answer your phone and help out with your accounts if you need time out of the office, or if you'd like to stop in at the nurse's station. You know how much I care about you and respect you, and of course we'll keep this just between us. We all have situations like this at times. Please don't feel bad or worry, I'm sure you'll find it's something that can be corrected.

Tip 198. Don't gossip. Because you respect the individual who has the hygiene problem, it is important to keep to a minimum any conversation about the person or the problem. Speculation, gossip, or just comparing notes are behaviors that are unproductive and can wind up hurting the person involved. Assume the problem will be corrected and the situation will be back to normal quickly, and take responsibility to help everyone to behave in a mature and graceful way.

Tip 199. If, after mentioning the problem to your team member the problem continues to affect your business efforts and does not seem to be going away, you may need to mention the situation to your manager or team leader (whoever would normally handle confidential personnel issues). He or she can then decide on the appropriate next step, and may choose to have a separate conversation with the person. Ultimately, any hygiene situation that adversely effects the team's ability to get its work done must be corrected.

Category: Interpersonal Problems
Problem: Gender or Racial Harassment

Tip 200. Develop and post a list of unacceptable behaviors. Consider both the spirit and the letter of the law. In many countries discrimination (or any different treatment) is illegal. These laws are important, and have been critical in the enforcement of equal treatment. The foundation of these laws, however, is just as important—the principle that everyone should have equal opportunity and be treated fairly. It is this fundamental belief, or value, that should guide our behavior toward others, whether they are in a legally protected class or not. This thinking can be traced back to what we've come to call the golden rule, which simply says "Do unto others as you would have them do unto you." Talk about this openly in team meetings and decide as a team what kind of behaviors will be acceptable and unacceptable in your team. Post this list in your team room.

Tip 201. Make antidiscrimination a job responsibility of each team member. Sometimes people act in biased ways simply because they don't realize they are doing it. Help them understand and accept personal responsibility for acting in ways that value diversity. Some actions that can be taken include:

- Regular discussion in team meetings about the importance of diversity, the need for individual perspectives in reviewing problems and creating plans, and the basic value held by the team that everyone should be treated with respect.

- Ensure that everyone gets equal chances to try new jobs, interact with customers, be considered for raises and promotions, and work together and lead committees.

- Deal with hurt feelings or offensive behavior, recognizing that these things are not to be taken lightly or trivialized.

- Identify discriminatory actions and suggest (or sometimes demand) different behaviors. Help team members understand that discriminatory behavior is unacceptable even if it is unintended.

- Invest in training for the team to help people recognize and change discriminatory behaviors.

- Treat discriminatory behaviors in the same way you would treat other unacceptable behaviors such as stealing, fighting, or breaking the law.

- Have someone on the team talk about what it feels like to be discriminated against. If this is too uncomfortable, bring in someone from outside of the team to talk to people about their experience.

Tip 202.   Have an operating guideline on mutual respect, equality, and/or diversity. Your team, when establishing guidelines, should have a discussion about your beliefs in this area and your commitment to nondiscrimination. Your team will not function effectively if discrimination blocks anyone's opportunity to contribute all of their talents to the team.

See Resource 2: Using Principles, Guidelines, and Boundaries

Tip 203.   Stand up for your rights as a citizen and as a team member. Each team member must be aware that no one has to tolerate different treatment based on race, gender, religion, disability, or age. We often come to genuinely care about our team members and work hard to foster a spirit of cooperation. You may be tempted to ignore discriminatory behaviors aimed at you. However, your team will not improve if you overlook these issues. Hopefully other members of the team will see what is happening and come to your aid. Unfortunately, however, that doesn't always happen. If you believe you may have been discriminated against by a team member or anyone else, please don't ignore your feelings. Cases of harassment should be reported to the proper authorities (usually the Human Resources department). You should know that:

- Your perceptions are important. It doesn't matter if someone "didn't mean it," or "didn't think you'd take it seriously." If someone else's behavior or workspace has offended you, you should pursue the resolution of the situation.

- A good first step is to talk to the person whose statement or action offended you. Let him or her know how you feel and that you don't want any further situations like this one. You can do this in a way that is not hurtful or punishing. You might say something like:

  > Sam, when you make jokes about women it makes me feel bad. You may not even realize that those jokes are offensive to me, so I thought I would tell you. Please stop.

- You should talk to your team leader about the situation. He or she is responsible for maintaining a discrimination-free workplace, and should support you and act as your ally. You may also get help from your Human Resources department. If the team leader is the problem, talk to them first. If this doesn't resolve the situation talk to your Human Resources representative.

- Remember that you don't need to explain why you feel the way you do, nor do you need to prove that the person who offended you meant to do so. You do need to state your feelings.

Tip 204.   It is very important for each team leader to be a role model in the area of nondiscrimination. A clear statement of values, behavior that is consistently sensitive to everyone being treated equally, and a firm position that discrimination will not occur in the team setting are essential.

See Resource 19: Team Leader Roles and Responsibilities
Resource 20: Being a Living Example

Tip 205.   Confront discrimination. If you witness a situation where discrimination exists, say something even if you are not personally involved. If you ignore it you become part of the problem. Sometimes, in fact, it is impossible for the person being treated unfairly to say much without being branded as overly sensitive. They need your help. You could say:

Joe, you just said some pretty unfair things to Fred about him not being able to do his job because he's "over the hill" and "getting senile," and you've said things like that to him before. You probably think you're funny and just kidding around, but if I were Fred it would really bother me. It's not funny, and I don't want you to treat him that way again. Please stop.

Category: Interpersonal Problems
Problem: Technical Problems

Tip 206. Involve both technical experts and other affected people in solving technical problems. Certain problems, for example, will require both lawyers and legal assistants, doctors and lab technicians, marketing people and sales representatives, or engineering and manufacturing people to work closely together even if they are not on the same natural work group team. When problems have been labeled "technical" and have been turned over exclusively to "technical" people, it leaves out many people who have critical data or who have a responsibility to act on whatever decision is made. As a rule of thumb include representatives of every group that must play a role in implementing the decisions made during the problem-solving process. If you do this you will make better decisions and people will feel more committed to carrying out the necessary improvements.

For example, assume that your company makes high-tech instrumentation and you discover that there has been a critical component failure in an instrument that is already in the hands of the customer. A team of people needs to get together to discuss the situation and its implications. This team would probably include:

- Vendors who make materials that went into the failing components.
- Lab technicians and operators who built the components.
- Engineers who designed the instrument.
- Sales people who sold the instruments to customers.
- Schedulers who will need to schedule in the corrected parts so no additional instruments get produced with this problem.
- Customer Service people who will need to go out to customer sites and replace the bad components with good ones.

- Marketing people who will need to write an announcement to the customers and develop a replacement program so that everyone has the least disruption possible.

The team should make decisions like:

- Who will do what?
- What is an acceptable timeline?
- Do we replace all components in instruments we've sold, or wait for customers to call to report a problem?
- Do we need to call in any outside experts?
- How can we come out of this with a stronger product and trust in our company name?

It is only by involving the entire team that all aspects of the situation will be thought through and the best possible solution will be implemented.

See Resource 12: Planning for Action

Tip 207.   Use the right problem-solving tools. Get data before you start suggesting solutions to a technical problem. Using certain problem-solving tools will help you clearly understand the problem. If you do this well, the solutions to the problem are often obvious. Without good, hard data, however, you can waste an enormous amount of time, money, and energy. If a piece of equipment isn't operating properly, for example, using the proper tools will help you isolate specific variables. Do more problems occur with one group of operators (potential training problem) when operating certain programs (potential software incompatibility), or under different environmental conditions (e.g., potential temperature, humidity, or dust problems)? The proper solution depends on a proper diagnosis. The right problem-solving tools will help establish patterns from which solutions emerge. Some examples of technical problem-solving tools include:

- Cause and Effect Diagrams
- Variance Analysis
- Pareto Analysis
- Weighted Criteria Worksheet

In addition, a technical problem may have some implications that are very important but are not technical. Sometimes, for example, the right solutions to certain technical problems are not implemented properly because of other people-related factors (like how to get others to agree to implement the solution). In those cases, it is helpful to use a tool focused on relationship issues, resource requirements, or other areas of nontechnical concern using the force-field analysis.

See Resource 11: Tools for Problem Solving

Tip 208. Stay technically current. Technology is advancing at an incredible rate, and just keeping current with the latest discoveries and products is a monumental task. But if you do, you will be able to think of more solutions to technical problems than you would otherwise. You will also be able to anticipate and resolve certain problems before they occur. Remember to:

- Read relevant technical journals for your operation.

- Have some team members visit technical shows from time to time.

- Invite in technical experts to give presentations. Find the best experts in your field, tell them as much as you can about what you do and how you do it, and listen to everything they have to say. Many companies have a "not invented here" syndrome, meaning they have little respect for things they didn't develop or customize to their own organization. Much can be learned from others. Don't forget to use resources from your customers and vendors.

- Visit other people with similar operations. Tours of other areas keep us from becoming content with our current thinking, and help us all to push ourselves to do things faster, better, cheaper, or to find a way not to eliminate nonessential work. In return, you can offer your hosts a visit to your site. Hoarding information is foolish in this day and age, because it becomes obsolete so quickly. There is generally more to lose by not talking to others than there is to gain by keeping everything secret.

Category: Interpersonal Problems
Problem: Lack of Authenticity or Honesty

Tip 209. Create a team environment that fosters openness. A key component of building and maintaining an effective team is the element of trust. Trust not only requires that we do what we say we'll do, but also that we tell the truth and are authentic with one another. Being authentic means maintaining a certain level of candor with team members and not censoring your own comments to either ensure that you don't make mistakes or to ensure that you'll be popular by not disagreeing with others. This is called having the "courage of your convictions," or having the strength to stand up for what you believe. This leads to healthy relationships and the best decisions for the business.

Sometimes people aren't authentic because they are nervous or timid about speaking out. They may not believe that they are as smart or knowledgeable as others on the team, or that they are senior enough yet to have opinions. This attitude, while very common, doesn't make the most of all the ideas of every team member. It leads to people worrying about how their comments will be perceived, rather than looking for solutions to business issues.

The best way to encourage people to be authentic in this kind of situation is to talk openly about the importance of everyone's ideas and perspectives. You might say:

> Roger, we know you're new here and haven't had any previous opportunity to be involved in selecting a vendor. You've said our process looks fine. However, we'd very much like to hear how you really feel about this situation— you bring to us the advantage of "new eyes," or, seeing a situation for the first time. Won't you give us your thoughts on the criteria for selection that we're working on?

At this point it is also very important that you then follow through and treat your team member's comments with respect. If you ridicule their observations or ignore them completely, you can bet that they won't be authentic the next time you ask for their opinions.

Tip 210. Confront a lack of candor. Sometimes team members are not authentic in situations because they are trying to either manipulate the process or the outcome. Motives may include personal gain (e.g., trying to get that new assignment) or a genuine concern for the benefit of the team (e.g., belief that the team doesn't see that their nominee would not be best for the job). Either way, this is not appropriate behavior in a team, and should be dealt with rather than ignored. There are a few ways to do this:

1. A positive approach is to have someone in charge of observing team process for all team meetings (you can even rotate this responsibility). This person would call a time out and make observations whenever the group process was unhealthy or nonproductive. This person would notice when group discussion did not seem to be completely genuine or open, and might suggest a different process at that moment to move things along.

2. Sometimes, the only way to move forward is to take a direct approach with the individual not being authentic. Try saying something like:

> Olga, I'm not sure you're giving us the whole story and telling us everything on your mind. Do you have some other concern that you haven't mentioned yet? We're all on this team together, and can't understand your position until we hear more.

Note: Just a note on people who attempt to manipulate the group process or the outcome: while these individuals usually believe they have a very clever and subtle approach, they are usually much more transparent to the group than they think.

3. If team members purposely distort the truth, this must be confronted. Lying cannot be tolerated in a team environment. Treat it as a performance problem. If you are unable to trust a team member because they do not tell the truth, your performance—and in some extreme cases, your safety—can be compromised. Do not tolerate it.

Tip 211. Strengthen communication skills. There are times when a team member appears to not be authentic when explaining his point of view. Perhaps that person does not have some of the basic communication skills needed to work effectively in a team. Everyone on the team should have some basic training in areas of communication. New members should automatically have the opportunity to attend core team training which includes communication skills and other skills and perspectives that are important for them to become a fully functional member of the team.

See Resource 13: Team Communication Basics

Category: Interpersonal Problems
Problem: Factions and Cliques

Tip 212. Look for opportunities to have people from different cliques work together on teamwide activities. Vary task teams, projects, shifts, and the like, so that over time everybody has an opportunity to work with everybody else. This personal experience will go a long way in helping people to work toward the common good, and in helping to reduce some of the natural conflict that occurs between groups (e.g., shifts, jobs, experience level, etc.).

Remember that factions and cliques are a part of everyday life. We all are drawn to people who are like ourselves, either physically, educationally, culturally, or in other ways. It is natural for people who are most comfortable with each other to gravitate toward each other, and develop comfortable and trusting relationships over time.

Help team members understand, however, that sometimes factions or cliques become destructive. They view loyalty to their faction as more important than loyalty to the team. They can often shut down lively debate by "road blocking" ideas they disagree with, and their ideas may be narrowly focused for the good of their clique in spite of what is best for the whole team.

To avoid some of these problems, consciously assign team members to projects and committees with others they usually are not aligned with. Over time, most people will have work experiences with many people on the team and this will tend to broaden their perspective on issues. It will also help them to be more receptive when new or diverse opinions are stated, because they will have had an opportunity to interact somewhat with the person who proposed the idea.

See Resource 14: Building a Collaborative Team Environment

Tip 213. Keep your focus on common ground: goals, results, and your team's charter. It is useful to review the team charter and to discuss as a group any alternatives for working together so that factions don't hinder your ability to accomplish your mission. Sometimes focusing on these issues that are important to everyone will cause people to rise above their special interests. Ultimately, of course, the factions cannot be allowed to get in the way of solid interpersonal relationships and smooth running processes. If the common ground focus doesn't work by itself, go into problem solving. After discussion and agreement that the situation must change, the team leader is responsible for making sure that team members follow through on their commitments. If that doesn't happen, this situation would be dealt with like any other performance issue.

Tip 214. Review the team charter and operating guidelines and act accordingly. One common way that teams react to peer pressure is to form cliques—groups of people who usually support each other regardless of the issue. While sometimes it can be comforting to know that there are people on your team who will always support you, it can be very destructive to the effort of the team as a whole. Whether you are a part of a clique, or you just observe that this process is beginning to occur, it is important to take responsibility to correct the situation. Some steps for solving this problem are to

- Acknowledge the existence of cliques and determine why they were created, what benefits they provide to people, and what their impact is on the team as a whole.

- Review the team charter and the needs of your customers at the next team meeting. As a group, determine whether the cliques make it more difficult to accomplish these objectives. If they do, team guidelines should be reviewed to see if there have been any group commitments made that, if followed, would solve the problem. If not, then it's appropriate to develop a new operating guideline together, carefully testing the final product to make sure that it really represents team members' commitments. A sample guideline might be:

  We will always work together as a team, and will deal with personal issues and preferences as they arise so that nothing gets in the way of the overall performance of the team in meeting customer needs.

- Come up with ways to address the needs people have that created the cliques in the first place.

See Resource 2: Using Principles, Guidelines, and Boundaries

Tip 215. Address unresolved conflict. Sometimes factions appear as a response to underlying conflict that is not resolved. As emotions get brought into situations, resentments may build and anger can develop, sometimes out of proportion to the situation that caused it. In these situations, it is important to acknowledge the cause and effect of this conflict in the team, and to productively deal with it. Symptoms include:

- Heated debate over issues.
- Subgroups or factions forming within the team.
- People feeling torn between allegiance to the team and allegiance to certain team members.

This is the time for the team to recognize the conflict. Team members should agree on a place, time, and process for resolving the conflict. A process that has been shown to work in such situations is:

- Acknowledge that the conflict exists.
- Identify the common ground that makes everyone want to resolve the conflict.
- Seek to understand all angles of the problem.
- Attack the issue side by side.
- Develop an action plan.

See Resource 15: Managing Team Conflict

   Category: Interpersonal Problems
   Problem: Peer Pressure

Tip 216. Say what you think even if it is different from what other powerful people have said. You might be right and they might be wrong. If you remain quiet when you disagree, you weaken the team's ability to make a good decision. Sometimes the team feels so much pressure from one or two team members to see an issue the same way they do, that team members will be hesitant to disagree with them or to suggest their own ideas. This can result in deferring to the team leader, or in agreeing to less than ideal team decisions to avoid any conflict with the assertive members. If you do this, you become disempowered. Avoid the temptation to do this. State your views. For example:

> We know that you both have very strong opinions that we should not involve engineers in purchasing materials for design projects. You said that we are the buyers, and have

years of experience getting the lowest price and the fastest delivery. You said that it is our job not theirs. However, I don't think that is what is best for our business. To start with, Angelica said that price, delivery, quality of material, and ability to be flexible over a long-term relationship are important to the engineers and that they would like to get involved in purchasing. I think that the engineers also need to understand better what we do here, and how changing designs midstream affects vendor relationships and cost. I'd like to include them.

See Resource 15: Managing Team Conflict

Tip 217. If certain people always tend to sway the opinions of others, try to change your decision-making process for a while. Try something called *nominal group technique*. Instead of starting with open debate on a topic, have everyone anonymously write down their opinion about the topic to be discussed on a piece of paper. Before any discussion have the meeting facilitator read all the opinions aloud before any discussion. This sometimes surfaces ideas that otherwise would be buried under the pressure of the opinion leaders.

Tip 218. Confront the peer pressure. If your team has fallen into a rut where one or two people seem to always get their way, then it may be time to do something to get everyone participating equally. You may say:

> You know, about half of us don't seem to be really fully participating in this discussion. It may be that Bill's solution is obviously the best one, but maybe we owe it to the business to make sure we review all the alternatives. I think we should each come up with one more idea that can improve what we've already agreed to.

Or:

> It seems to me that we've been taking the easy way out and relying on Jim and Ed to lead the way again. I'd like to see all of us take a more active role in helping to make decisions in our team. We owe it to our customers. I'll start . . . .

If the kind of peer pressure you are encountering is hurtful to particular individuals, watch it closely. Peer pressure can actually be positive if it focuses everyone on gently prodding each other to do what is best for your customers and business. But if it results in team members being discriminated against, harassed, or ignored, it must be confronted more strongly than

the examples demonstrate. In those cases treat it as a performance problem. Clearly state the expectation that these pressur-
ing behaviors stop. If they don't, ask for help from your team
leader.

    Category: Interpersonal Problems
    Problem: Compliance

Tip 219.   Evaluate comments and recommendations based
on their own merit and not on who says them. One of the most
dangerous problems teams can run into is thoughtless compli-
ance to powerful people. A fundamental assumption about the
effectiveness of teams is that a decision discussed and affirmed
as a group will usually be better than a decision made by a
single person. This is because the combined knowledge and
experiences of the group is greater than any individual (except,
of course, in certain rare, highly technical situations where
only a few experts understand the situation). Sometimes, however, an individual on the team will make the mistake of seeing
decisions as choosing between people instead of choosing
between options. He may believe that disagreeing with a
friend, corporate staff member, union executive, or with the
team leader is disloyal ("If you really respected me you would
support me."). In a team it is important to do what is best
regardless of who suggests the different alternatives being
evaluated.

Tip 220.   Value diversity. Team members should remember that diversity within the team makes it stronger, even if
there may be uncomfortable times when people disagree with
each other. Work it through. When many points of view are
discussed before an agreement is reached, you will get a better
solution with deeper team commitment to implement it.
    Some indicators that tell you that your team needs to im-
prove its ability to value diversity include:

- Factions or cliques that begin to form on the team according
  to common styles, opinions, friendships, or backgrounds.

- Certain members who are becoming alienated because they
  tend to be different in one way or another.

- New ideas or points of view that are often rejected because
  they do not fit with the team's established way of doing
  things.

- The team members who tend to follow the lead of those who are more vocal or who enjoy the most popularity, overlooking those who are less vocal or whose point of view might be difficult to understand.
- Team members who make jokes—subtle or explicit—that discredit minority opinions, styles, or characteristics.

See Resource 14: Building a Collaborative Team Environment

Tip 221. Don't avoid conflict. Many people think of conflict as negative, and associate it with arguing, fighting, and anger. But if conflict is managed properly, it will become a productive way to compare the merit of one idea with another, resulting in the strongest possible business decisions. Conflict exists because:

- People care.
- People are different.
- People are interdependent.
- People have expectations.

These same four points also characterize the most committed and innovative teams. To make your team a success, your responsibility is to use conflict in a constructive and positive way for the benefit of the team. Some steps you can take to manage conflict within the team are to

- Recognize that you are experiencing conflict within the team.
- Develop a one sentence statement that you believe describes the problem
- Bring this statement to the team and get your team members help in refining the statement so that it reflects everyone's perception of the situation.
- Ask for everyone to develop a plan together to correct the situation and to take responsibility to help solve the problem.

See Resource 15: Managing Team Conflict

Category: Interpersonal Problems
Problem: Deference

Tip 222. Avoid deferring to the same one or two people all the time. It is not uncommon, for example, for team members to respond to what the team leader says as if it is more important than comments from others. In this case, you may ask the team leader, or other person who is normally deferred to, not to state his or her opinion until near the end of the team discussion. If you are the person normally deferred to, listen to the ideas of others carefully and thoughtfully, and seek out good points to support when others talk. Emphasize that your ideas are just one more opinion for the team to consider. Over time, an environment of respect for ideas and equality will be created. To encourage more equal participation the team leader might say things like:

> I liked what Janine had to say a lot. The concept of asking the Finance department to create a new and simpler report for us that would come out weekly is a great idea, and I hadn't thought of it myself. What if we asked Janine and Merle to meet with Finance to share their suggestion and to get other ideas from them?

> You know, I thought I'd come up with a workable approach to scheduling the work through the process area to meet our deadline. I was hoping we could borrow two technicians from wafer fab to fill out our swing shift, and that the extra capacity would get us done with only a little overtime. But now that I've found out they have nothing to spare, I thought we could discuss this as a team to get some other alternatives. Betty, haven't you been faced with this situation before?

Tip 223. Brainstorming can effectively disconnect an idea from a particular individual and create a feeling of team responsibility for suggestions. This process frees up team members to think creatively. It also minimizes the problem of people deferring to one individual. To start a modified form of brainstorming that helps with deference problems, the group restates what the issue or problem is and then reviews the rules as follows:

- We will ask for ideas from each person as we go around the table. If you have nothing you want to suggest, say "pass" and we move on to the next person. We will continue to go around the table until we run out of ideas or time.

- Questions can only be asked during brainstorming to clarify what is meant by the idea. There can be no comments about how any idea is either good or bad. Even crazy ideas are okay. They might cause somebody else to think of something that they might not have considered otherwise. Every comment is important and will be listed on a chartpad by the facilitator so everyone can see all the ideas at all times.

- Anyone can build off anyone else's previous comment and expand or modify a comment to become a new comment.

- After going around the table until everyone says "pass," or after the specified time period is up, discussion of the ideas begins. Ideas can be grouped into "workable," "might work," and "probably won't work." This way, no one is tied to a particular idea because everyone has generated several of them. Any solution agreed to will be the product of everyone's thinking.

Tip 224. Eliminate favorites. There are times when a team defers consistently to one person's opinion because that person usually gets support from the team leader. They feel that since this person will usually get their way anyway, it is futile to offer any different suggestions. This is unhealthy and needs to be corrected.

This person may be the most senior, have the highest level job, or have some critical and unique skill. Or sometimes, the reasons that the team leader supports this person are more political (e.g., the person is friends with an influential person in the company, the person socializes with the manager or team leader, or the person has taken on the role of a "yes person"). Whatever the specifics of the situation, the responsibility lies with the team leader to always behave in a fair and impartial way. Being perceived to have favorites will not only serve to disrupt the activities of the team, but will ultimately lead to team members having less respect for the team leader. If you find yourself in this situation advise your team leader openly and honestly. You might say:

> Maria, I noticed this morning that you supported Alice's proposal for planning the customer feedback session. I know Alice has good ideas from time to time but it seems you support her a lot more than you support others. That makes me not want to say anything in meetings. I figure 'why bother?,' because whatever Alice says is normally what you are going to support whether it is really the best idea or not. I believe this is harming our team. I need your

help to improve the situation. It's not right and it violates our operating guidelines.

Category: Interpersonal Problems
Problem: Yes-Teams

Tip 225. Be patient and learn from your mistakes. New teams often take on more responsibilities than they can successfully complete. They want to do a good job. When teams are first formed, they are trying to understand their new roles and team charter, participate in the creation of guidelines, listen to the boundary conditions given to them, and continue to produce a superior product or provide a high-quality service. This is like trying to ride a bicycle and change the tire at the same time.

During this time, teams often have a tendency to say "yes" to everything. Individuals are used to being told what to do, and switching over to being actively involved in some of the decisions is a difficult personal challenge. Remember that part of being involved is knowing when to say "no." It doesn't help anyone if the team volunteers for projects or other responsibilities that they are unable to complete as expected. Over time you will learn to judge your team's work capacity better as you come to appreciate the full scope of your new responsibilities. Team leaders should not lose patience with new teams, but see this as an opportunity to help them to become comfortable with their responsibilities and roles at a sensible pace.

Tip 226. Get better information and analysis tools. Sometimes teams say "yes" to everything because they are unaware of what they don't know. For example, they aren't aware of the questions they should be asking to determine whether they should accept particular assignments, where to go for relevant information, or which experienced people they might ask for advice.

Teams that are ignorant of these facts don't really have any choice but to say "yes" to any request that sounds good, whether the request comes from inside or from outside the team. But good decision making requires that you make educated choices. To accept additional responsibilities the teams should at least have some basic information about the implications of this decision. To get this information you might ask questions like:

- What do we need to do to complete this successfully?
- What is the likely return or desired result of this project?
- How much time, money, resources, or other types of investments will it take?
- Does the customer require this?
- How long will we need to perform these tasks (temporarily, permanently)?
- How will accepting this responsibility affect the other priorities we have?

In this situation, the team leader plays a key role as coach in setting up experiences and discussions to help the team provide training for team members in decision making, problem solving, and analysis tools.

See Resource 3: Making Group Decisions
Resource 10: Team Problem Solving
Resource 11: Tools for Problem Solving

Tip 227. Learn the right way to say "no." Sometimes, teams that say "yes" to everything because they don't know how to say "no." They are worried about the consequences of disagreeing with the team leader or other powerful people either inside or outside of the team. They may be afraid of hurting their careers, or they may be trying to impress other people. But saying "yes" to something you can't do will ultimately backfire and cause others to lose respect and confidence in the team. There are ways to say no that are polite and reasonable. Don't say: "No, we don't want to do that," or "No, that's a bad (stupid, naive, etc.) idea." This approach can be offensive. Instead say something like:

Hans, unfortunately we don't have the resources to do what you have requested at this time. If you can help us get more resources we will obviously reconsider. We would need two more people for six weeks.

Or:

If we take on this responsibility we will need to eliminate the XYZ project. We feel that project is more important to our customers than this request.

If we say that team members are a part of the decision-making process and then get annoyed when they don't accept all of our suggestions or requests, we are being dishonest. It is the team leaders responsibility to provide a safe environment for the discussion and solution of problems, and for her behavior to always emphasize that the target is to determine the best thing for the business. The team leader must hold herself responsible for providing a consistently fair, results-focused environment where ideas are discussed on their merit. Individual loyalties and biases have no place in this kind of discussion.

Category: Interpersonal Problems
Problem: New Team Members

Tip 228. Use a good, participative hiring process. It is important, when faced with the prospect of bringing in a new team member, to have a clear and well-understood process that everyone involved understands. Up front, a decision must be made to decide who will be involved in the effort, and exactly what skills and areas of strength your team needs. Remember to determine which laws or policies may affect hiring decisions in your organization (normally, your Human Resources representative will know this). Often, it is helpful for one team member to lead this project, who will take responsibility for ensuring that all the jobs get done on time. This person may say:

> I'd like all of us to work together to select just the right person to join our team. I know we need the new person to be on board in six weeks, and I have put together a rough project plan to show the steps we need to get done between now and then. Let's discuss this together right now to see if we all agree on this process, and then we can volunteer for the areas where we'd like to participate. When we're done, we can take this to our team leader for his input.

Using a process like this helps you make a better decision about who to hire and also make it easier for the new team member to come on board successfully. They will already have met some (or all) of the team members, and the people who participate in the selection process will be more likely to support the new team member when she arrives.

See Resource 18: Selecting Team Members

Tip 229. Provide an effective new team member orienta- tion. Once you have selected your new team member, it is important to make sure that that person gets off to a good start. The team should discuss what kinds of information that per- son will need, and what training will help to give him the skills he'll need for success. Usually, areas to be covered will include:

- A good understanding of the team charter.
- His role within the group.
- Thorough awareness of the group's customers, competitors, and suppliers.
- The group boundaries and guidelines.
- Usual group processes (like weekly team meetings to review work flow, and so on).
- Skills needed (technical skills, business skills, and interper- sonal team skills such as effective meeting skills, consensus decision making, basic communication skills, and the like).

Assign this new person a "mentor," someone he can ask any questions of, and who will take personal responsibility for showing him around and introducing him to others. Have your certified trainer schedule time to work with him in new skill areas. Remember that this new person will not feel as strongly as you and other team members do about the importance of things like the boundaries and charter if he didn't help to create them. Involve him as quickly as possible in other group decisions to help him get a sense of ownership in the team decisions.

See Resource 3: Making Group Decisions
Resource 6: Holding Effective Meetings
Resource 13: Team Communication Basics

Tip 230. Be patient and supportive. It is very important to remember that every new person will need time to get used to working in a team environment. Just as it took many months to develop your team and your roles, it will require time and patience on everyone's part to integrate any new person into your team. She will probably be used to being told what to do, and may be hesitant to offer suggestions for fear that it is not her job to do that. Team members can help out greatly by gently reminding her of how things are done, being good role models, and giving constructive and helpful feedback as situations come up.

If you notice that the new person does not contribute ideas in a team meeting, you can say:

> Sue, we've been tossing around some ideas on how we can make it easier for our customers to work with us. Right now, they call one person for sales and another for any changes in their service contract, and a third for any repairs to be made. You've got quite a bit of experience as an account manager and we're anxious to get your perspective on this concept. How do you feel about the idea of account teams to give customers one point of contact?

Category: Interpersonal Problems
Problem: Team Leader Changes

Tip 231. Involve the team in making decisions about new team leaders. A team leader is an important and integral part of any team. When that person moves on to another job it has a profound affect on the team. If the wrong replacement comes in, a team can be destroyed. Every team is influenced by the style of a leader, and if that style is either too autocratic or too permissive, the teams productivity, morale, and effectiveness will be seriously reduced. To minimize this possibility, include the team in selecting the next team leader.

Team members should determine what leadership skills are most important and what values the leader will need to have to be supportive. Generate a list of desirable qualities, skills and values. Discuss these thoroughly, and try to reduce the number of criteria to a manageable number (probably not more than 10). It is usually not too difficult to find the 10 most important areas.

Next, the group should decide if any of these are absolute "musts" for the candidate. An example might be "belief in a team-based environment." These criteria should be considered required minimums and any person who does not meet these should not be considered for the position. Then, the team should review the remaining criteria, and weight them from 1 to 10 as to importance in this position.

By using these few elements in a matrix format, each candidate can be scored 1 to 10 in each of the criteria.

Each person interviewing should be given a copy of the criteria, and should participate in a discussion about the criteria selection, weighted importance, and the "musts" that have been outlined. It is important that consensus be reached about each element of this document.

Interviews should be held (either one-on-one or several with the candidate at once), where predetermined questions are asked, along with questions that seem logical based on the conversation that takes place. Remember to ask open-ended questions (not questions that can be answered with simple yes or no responses) and rely heavily on past experience, not on what the candidate says they will do in the future. Instead of asking: "Do you like team-based organizations?" for example, instead ask things like:

Can you give us an example of where you worked in a team-based operation? What did you like most and like least about your experience?

When the interviews are complete, the interviewers get together to review their findings and discuss their opinions (this is called a *debrief*).

At this point the team will look at each persons score on the interview worksheets you developed. Multiply the score by the ranking for each criteria. If, for example you rated "experience in a team environment" a 9 and you gave the individual you interviewed a 9 on that criterion, the score would be 81 for that candidate on that criterion. This allows you to compare total scores for all candidates who met all the "musts" criteria.

This process feels scientific, but it just gives the interview team a general picture of the relative appropriateness of each of the interviewees. It is only through thorough discussion and a little bit of "gut feel" that everyone will agree on the right new team leader. Rank the interviewees and give your input to the other people who are participating in the job selection process (normally senior management and Human Resources representatives).

Tip 232. Keep a positive attitude. The loss of the team leader is a difficult time for any team. It will cause reflection on roles and processes currently in place, and there will probably be speculation about what it will be like without her. This kind of change is difficult to deal with, and can cause significant stress and anxiety for some individuals. It is important for the team to pull together at this time, and remind each other that there is nothing productive to be gained from speculation. There is no reason to believe that the next team leader won't be as effective or caring. Perhaps a change in approach might turn out to be a good thing.

Being involved in selecting the next leader will really help the transition process, but it is not always possible. Some tips during this transition include:

- Not believing anything you've heard about the person who will be working with you soon. It's only someone's opinion at another point in time in another situation.

- Keeping your focus on the business and your charter in meeting the customers' needs. It is far too easy to get side-tracked into putting energy into worry and second-guessing the future.

- Not waiting to be asked if you have some strong input about your needs or your situation. Set up some time with the hiring manager (your team leader's manager) to present your comments and request consideration.

- Keeping a positive attitude. Odds are even that the new team leader will work out well. Everyone deserves a fair chance.

Tip 233. Provide a good orientation for the new team leader. As soon as the new team leader is on board, the team should do its best to provide an orientation to the way things are working now. Welcome the new team leader to the team with a presentation that includes details about the team charter, operating guidelines, and boundary conditions and information about the teams customers and suppliers. Talk about current processes, roles, and responsibilities. Finally, review your goals and accomplishments.

Talk about ways the team might partner with the new leader to help him get up to speed as easily and quickly as possible.

Tip 234. Handle promotions with sensitivity and honesty. In the event that the new team leader was promoted from the team, the situation is a little more difficult. Sometimes there are jealousies because other team members believe they were just as qualified for the position as the new team leader, sometimes there is cynicism because other team members remember the flaws and inadequacies of the new leader, and sometimes it is just awkward to treat your former peer as a team leader. Often these situations are so difficult that it is best for the team and for the team leader to transfer the promoted team member to lead a different team. This will give everybody a fresh start. If this is not appropriate, the best approach may be a direct one, where the new team leader says:

> Hello, everyone. I must admit that I am pleased to have been selected as your team leader, but I also recognize that this is a somewhat uncomfortable situation right now. I want to be clear up-front about the fact that I believe strongly in this team, and am proud of everything we have accomplished over the years we've had together. I certainly don't claim to have answers to all our problems, and I can state without a doubt that I know I never will. What made us successful was the partnership we had with each other and with Stan, the previous team leader. I want to continue that tradition, and request that you ask me to provide the same kinds of facilitating, barrier busting, and support that he did.

Category: Interpersonal Problems
Problem: Layoffs

Tip 235. If possible create a "rings of defense" strategy to deal with bad times. Hopefully you will never need to use your strategy, but a reality of current work life is that sometimes, even if you do your best, your organization has financial problems that will require sacrifices to allow the operation to survive. It is a little easier to take if you help decide what will happen in this situation. This strategy should be developed far before you ever need it. It will include a series of progressive actions that will be taken in lean times such as an elimination of bonuses, shared days off without pay, or salary cuts if the business takes a downturn. Remember to work through the proper management, union, or government channels for approval during these discussions. Ask for help from your Human Resources representative. Realize that in some organizations creating rings of defense may be outside your boundary conditions.

Downsizing in a team environment should be used only as a last resort. The emotional damage both to the people who are laid off and to the survivors of the layoff can be seriously debilitating. This damage can hinder a team's effectiveness for months afterward.

Tip 236. Provide emotional support to people who will be laid off. No matter how logical we try to be in understanding that layoffs are sometimes necessary and are not a reflection on an individual's performance on the job, any time someone leaves a position involuntarily it is a painful and emotional process. It's important that team members recognize this as they interact with the person who'll be leaving. Most importantly, do not avoid the laid off individual because you are uncomfortable or don't know what to say. Simple but heartfelt comments work well. Say something like: "Shana, I just heard you were getting laid off, and I don't know what to say. I feel really bad about it. I'll miss working with you a lot."

Your job as a team member is to be honest (you may say how you feel, but need not say anything you don't believe). Be supportive (offer any support or help that you are comfortable with—sometimes, saying, "Call me if you want to talk," is all that can be offered) but don't assume responsibility for decisions that weren't yours (if the company's financial downturn was out of your hands, and if decisions were made without team member input, these areas are not your responsibility). Do take responsibility for decisions that were yours (suggestions or comments that team members contributed are always used in the context of business decisions, and may ultimately have helped to delay the layoff, or make it less severe).

Tip 237. Don't gossip or speculate. Recognize that the temptation is strong to embellish the facts with speculation. In the long run, this speculation is disruptive and nonproductive, and can begin a swirl of negative talk throughout the area. Help to deter this gossip by not participating in the speculation yourself. Also, you can provide some solid coaching when approached by someone by saying:

> All we really know is that Shana was let go. We have no reason to believe that there are more layoff announcements to come, or that Shana won't be called back as soon as the work picks up. Right now, I'm going to concentrate on getting as much done as I can to avoid the company having to take further action.

Category: Interpersonal Problems
Problem: Low Team Energy

Tip 238. Infuse business information into the team. Often teams become increasingly focused on their tasks and activities and take less time to maintain their understanding of their whole business and their customers as they grow older. This can result in an increasing concern with day-to-day fire fighting with a decreasing emphasis on the big picture. The daily fire fighting becomes monotonous and stressful.

To improve and or avoid these situations keep in touch with your customers and other major ongoing changes in your business environment. Ways to keep the team energized include:

- Once a month bringing a representative from a customer group (internal or external) to a team meeting to talk about how they use the team's products, and ways that the team might improve or simplify processes.

- Brainstorming a list of key competitors for the company or the team's processes/products, and assign one to each team member to become familiar with. Watching local newspapers for press releases, reading trade journals for new developments, collecting promotional materials, talk to others in that industry, attending trade shows, and if possible purchasing your competitors product or service to better understand how it stacks up with yours.

- As a team, reviewing your company's business plan and strategy over the next year or so. Benchmarking your team against others in your field, looking for ways to improve, simplify, or innovate to ensure you stay competitive in technology and cost.

- Bringing top managers from your business to a team meeting to discuss their personal visions, their needs from your group in the future, and to answer any questions your group may have.

Tip 239. If you feel low energy because you're tired, brainstorm ideas to increase energy. Especially after lots of overtime or weekend work, teams can get in a low energy rut. It seems like the team is just running in place and not making much progress. Recognize the symptoms of very low energy (heading toward burnout) and call a meeting to get the team back on track.

> Hey, do you realize that most of us haven't had any time with our families to speak of for seven weeks now? Sure, we're committed to meeting our goals, but a half an hour of discussion and brainstorm might get us out of this burnout cycle.

Steps can be taken to analyze the situation and solve it:

- As a team, develop a concise problem statement to define the situation (e.g., since Joe and Elaine left, we've all been working overtime nonstop to meet our objectives).

- List ideas on a chartpad that might solve the problem (e.g., find out if we can hire a replacement for either person who left, explore whether other teams in the company have individuals we could borrow, see if any process steps could be temporarily subcontracted until the situation is back to normal, renegotiate team goals, and force ourselves to take some vacation time before we burn out).

Tip 240.   Create learning opportunities. An important way to maintain high energy in a team is to ensure that people have an opportunity to constantly improve their skills and knowledge. A team whose members have a large variety of skills is also much more flexible in dealing with new situations (or deadline crises) than one with individuals who can each do only one or two jobs. Raising individual energy will result in higher team energy. Some ways to plan for continuous skill growth include the ability to:

- Think of every team member as a trainer, with responsibilities to share their knowledge and techniques with others. Schedule events for team members to teach others some of their special skills or to pass along tips they have learned.

- Have different team members try out new responsibilities (even though it may take a little longer or affect productivity at first) when planning workload and output.

- Provide positive feedback to those willing to try new things, and don't punish individuals when mistakes are made in a new job—this is the way we grow and learn.

- Provide positive feedback to those willing to share their expertise with others.

- Create personal development plans for each team member. Include the things to be learned over a one-year period, and the resources required (e.g., training, time, tuition reimbursement, etc.).

- Create learning contracts with each other. These contracts might include agreements on how to learn from mistakes, how to facilitate cross training, and plans for the schedules and budget necessary to learn new skills.

- Take advantage of college courses offered in your community.

- Schedule other teams from your organization to come in and give your team a presentation on what they are doing (special project status, etc.).

Category: Interpersonal Problems
Problem: Creating Trust

Tip 241. Make personal commitments to do the things that create trust. Trust is a crucial component of any productive team. It is slow to develop and easy to lose, and requires everyone's effort. Remember, the only way to get trust is to give trust. As an individual, you should make the following commitments to your fellow team members:

- Be open and honest.

- Work to eliminate conflicts of interests.

- Do what you say you will do.

- Avoid talking behind each other's backs.

- Trust your teammates.

- Give team members the benefit of the doubt and assume that their intentions are good.

See Resource 14: Building a Collaborative Team Environment

Tip 242. Separate unhealthy emotion from work activities. Teams invariably get involved in stressful issues that tempt team members to get emotional. While some emotion is predictable and healthy, some manifestations of emotion will damage relationships and weaken trust among team members. The following tips will help you to always treat others with respect:

- Do not lose your temper.

- Do not put others down.

- Do not call names.

- Never be physically abusive, even in jest.

- Do not blame or embarrass others.

- Do not lie.

- Do not ridicule other peoples ideas, beliefs, or actions.

See Resource 14: Building a Collaborative Team Environment

Tip 243. If you recognize the symptoms of eroded trust, talk about it openly. When you find yourself in a situation where trust does not exist, you will see some of the following indicators:

- Team members find it difficult to share honest feelings.
- People withhold information.
- There is a tendency for team members to place blame and criticize.
- You feel a need to cover your tracks.
- People are talking behind the backs of others.

If any of these symptoms exist, confront the specific situation and get the team back on track. You could say:

Our guidelines say we will discuss concerns with the individual involved, instead of complaining to a friend or talking behind each other's backs. I remember when we all committed to do that—we said things like:

- "Nothing will ever get fixed until the person you have a concern about is given a chance to fix it."
- "If someone had a problem with me, I'd sure want to hear about it directly and not through the grapevine."
- "It's important we all commit to this, because we know we'll be a better team for it (even though we also know it will take guts to bring up things directly)."

We are doing just what we said we wouldn't. I'd like to call a time out and get us recommitted to doing this right. Let's talk this through, make sure we still buy into this guideline now that we know how tough it is to follow, and resolve to do better.

Category: Interpersonal Problems
Problem: Drugs or Alcohol

Tip 244. Focus on fixing the behavior, don't speculate about the cause. Sometimes we begin to notice nontypical behavior on the part of another individual. We might ignore it until the same erratic behavior surfaces again. At that time, it's very tempting to jump to a conclusion that the individual is using drugs or alcohol, and to feel a sense of urgency about getting the situation resolved.

The first rule in these situations is to observe the behavior, but not to diagnose the cause. Leave that to a professional. It's not unheard of for erratic behavior to result from something like two prescription medicines interacting with each other, sleep deprivation, depression, or some physical illnesses like Tourette's syndrome or epilepsy. Describe the behavior to the person and ask them if they need help (it's possible you could phone a doctor, or help out in some other way). You should also report the incident to your team leader.

Tip 245. If you see someone behaving unsafely (stumbling and falling, falling asleep on the job, threatening someone else, and the like), get the person off the job site before an injury or serious accident occurs. You don't have to prove they are under the influence, or accuse them of using drugs or alcohol—you just need to tell them they are behaving unsafely. Usually, you can get your team leader to take care of this. Call a taxi cab or find another appropriate way to safely take the person home (allowing the person to drive under those conditions is unwise, and a cab is usually a handy alternative). Unless you have other policies or guidelines, the person should normally be paid for the rest of their shift, and should come in the next day at the start of their workday to meet with the team leader.

Tip 246. Make expectations clear. During a discussion about operating guidelines or a similar topic, talk about using drugs or alcohol at work. Emphasize that the team will not dictate what is morally right or wrong, nor tell people what they should or shouldn't do outside work. But teams do need to develop guidelines for acceptable behavior while at work. Some of these things may already be part of established policy. In addition to giving everyone a clear understanding of whatever the expectations are (virtually all teams do not allow people to work under the influence of nonprescription drugs or alcohol for safety, legal, or insurance reasons), reassure them that the team is sensitive to the fact that dependency is a disease that can be successfully treated. That means that even though it's unacceptable to come to work under the influence, people will be offered a pathway to get help, not condemnation from their team members.

Tip 247. Get the team leader involved immediately. While no one, not even the team leader, can accuse someone of taking drugs or using alcohol based solely on watching their behavior, any suspicion that this is occurring should be viewed as a serious situation and handled immediately. At a minimum these behaviors can hurt the effectiveness of the team, and if the behavior is alcohol or drug related it can be life-threatening if it causes safety problems.

Usually, the team leader will sit down with the person and have a conversation that includes examples of the inappropriate behavior, a clear statement that this behavior is unacceptable and will be cause for disciplinary action if not corrected immediately, and a statement of company policy related to alcohol and drug use in the event that the person needs help in this area. That conversation might go like this:

> Clint, I'm afraid I need to talk to you about some performance issues I've observed over the last couple of weeks. I've had two of your teammates come to me with concern for you, and I've observed some erratic and unsafe things that you've done. Those include: last Friday after lunch I saw your head nodding while you were at your machine, your eyes drooped closed and you kept them closed and appeared to be asleep for more than 10 minutes. Also, after break Tuesday you came in and started criticizing Elaine, and raised your voice to the point where I thought you were going to take a swing at her. You sometimes slur your speech, and your sentences and logic don't always make sense—like in that meeting you participated in to review last week's parts shortages. In addition, you have been late the last three Mondays.
>
> Clint, I need to tell you that this behavior is unacceptable, and you've been gone more than the team can cover for you. We all need to depend on each other here. Also, safety is a critical issue in any area with heavy machinery, and any safety infraction must be dealt with according to company policy. If I see any more evidence of this behavior, I will need to write you up and start the progressive discipline process.
>
> If this behavior is related in any way to any other issue, I do want to remind you that we believe that alcoholism and drug dependency are diseases that can be treated, and the company will support you if you believe this, or any other health issue, is part of the problem and want to seek

treatment. However, I am certainly not qualified to say that I believe this is true, and am only letting you know about our company policies in case they will help.

In this situation, it is the team member's responsibility to either correct his behavior on his own or to identify that he needs help to correct his behavior.

Tip 248. Help people who need help. If your team member comes to you and confides that she has a drug or alcohol problem, it is very tempting to agree not to tell anyone. This seems like something a true friend would do for another friend. But if this dependency has shown up in any way at work, the person is jeopardizing the rest of the team at the same time. Keeping this secret does your friend no good. Encourage her to get some help. This is too big of a battle to fight by oneself.

It is most responsible to tell your friend that what you'd like to do is go with her to talk to the team leader about the situation, and to jointly find out her options for working on the problem. While it's probably not going to be something the other person will want to do, with a little bit of logic and a lot of reassurance that she won't be ridiculed (and will actually get help and support), some people will agree to this plan.

For those who don't agree to ask for help, it almost always makes sense to tell them how serious the whole team views this kind of situation and that you feel like you must go to the team leader. This is the time for tough love. If you can't find a way to help your friend see how serious these kinds of problems are, you're not a real friend at all. At a minimum, encourage them to talk to health professionals. The professionals will then normally make sure the team leader is informed of the treatment process so that your friend can get the help she needs.

Tip 249. If you happen to come upon someone using alcohol or drugs on the job, or find them at your workplace, it is important to tell the team leader. Almost every company has strict written policies about drug and alcohol use, and they must be adhered to in order to protect everyone's safety and to guarantee a quality product. Most teams will have talked about situations like this in guidelines and values discussions, so it will not come to anyone as a surprise that you feel strongly about correcting this situation. In cases where you are a witness, it is your responsibility to come forward with the information you have.

Usually the team leader will then confront the individual and say that she knows that drugs or alcohol have been used on the job site, and the situation will be managed according to company policy.

Category: Meetings
Problem: Lengthy Decisions

Tip 250. Write the main discussion points down on a chartpad or board. It can be frustrating to take a long time to make decisions. Try this: When making a difficult decision with fellow team members, write down key points during the discussion on a chartpad everyone can see. By writing them down, it is then easier to review the best ideas and discard the worst. This leads to a quicker decision on the point being discussed. Say something like:

> Let's have one person write the key discussion points down on the chartpad as we discuss this decision. Thank you, Marie, for taking that on today. I'll do it next time.

See Resource 6: Holding Effective Meetings

Tip 251. Use voting if you can't come to a true consensus. Normally consensus decision making is preferable for teams. In consensus, a team will come to a decision that everyone can support even if it isn't everyone's first choice. But sometimes teams get blocked and can't reach consensus. If so, try taking a vote. Realize that the people who are outvoted will probably not support the outcome. By having a reasonable discussion with everyone participating, however, a vote of the team will lead to a decision most people like and can live with. Avoid doing this on really important decisions. Take the time to talk those out. Also avoid unanimous decision making disguised as consensus. In a difficult decision an unanimous decision cannot be reached in a reasonable time. To take a vote you might say:

> I see we have been taking a lot of meeting time on this discussion and decision. Let's take a vote on the two best ideas so far.

See Resource 3: Making Group Decisions

Tip 252. Use a process called team polling for a decision after a long discussion. *Team polling* is a nonbinding vote that allows people to say what decision they would make now based on the information they have so far. It can help people get back on track especially in situations when the decision continues to drag on and team members seem to become repetitive. Many times people are trying hard to convince each other of things they may already have agreement on. Check it out. To run the polling say:

> I see we have been going over and over several points for quite awhile now. Perhaps we should go around the table and see what everyone would do if they had to make the decision right now. If we agree, we'll go on to the next point on our agenda. If not, we'll keep talking. I'll start. I think we should go with Janet's plan. Bob, you're next, how do you feel?

Tip 253. Use time limits and summaries. To speed up the decision, try to determine a time limit for a certain discussion. Then make the decision based on what you have talked about to that point. One team member or facilitator should pull together the data already discussed and summarize it prior to the decision. A way to clarify time limits and summarize information might sound like this:

> We have been on this topic of discussion for a long time now. How about if I try to summarize the key thoughts and then we allow about 10 more minutes of discussion. Then we will move on to the decision. Is that okay with everybody?

See Resource 3: Making Group Decisions

Category: Meetings
Problem: Starting Late

Tip 254. Meet at the same time every team meeting. Whether it is a daily or monthly meeting, the easiest way for team members to consistently come to the meetings on time is to make it a habit. Starting at the same time will soon become easier for all the team members to remember. If possible, use the same room, this also keeps the team from wondering where the meeting is being held. The team leader should always set an example of promptness.

See Resource 6: Holding Effective Meetings

Tip 255.   Have a specific team member responsible for announcing the meeting to the group. This often works well in an area where fellow team members are close at hand and a friendly "five minutes until our scheduled meeting time" reminder is most helpful, whether it is by voice or electronic mail. The job of reminder should rotate so each team member has the shared responsibility. A reminder might sound like this:

> Remember team ... we are scheduled to begin our morning meeting in about five minutes in conference room A.

Tip 256.   Reevaluate team commitment and charter. When a team becomes unfocused about meeting times, they are usually unfocused about the purpose of the meetings as well. Sometimes it is helpful to have a team discussion about the commitment made, to make these meetings successful and timely. A discussion lead-in might be:

> I see we are becoming consistently later with our start times. Our focus around these team meetings seems to have changed. Let's have a candid discussion today about our attitude about meetings. Are they still important for us?

See Resource 6: Holding Effective Meetings

Tip 257.   Come up with a gimmick that everybody agrees with. Some teams make late members pay a fine each time they are late. This money is later used for a team party. Others politely applaud when late members show up. They'll get the message. Remember that sometimes people may have good business related reasons for tardiness (e.g., being on the phone with a customer). Whatever you come up with should be gentle.

Category: Meetings
Problem: Too Many Meetings

Tip 258.   Have efficient well-run meetings. Sometimes people complain of too many meetings because the meetings they attend are ineffective. Team members will not complain if the meetings are meaningful to the work at hand. If a meeting is organized and to the point, it will help rather than hinder getting the work done. A way of encouraging teammates to attend might be to say:

Today's meeting will be a brief, important one. We will look specifically at how the new telephone voice mail system affects our service.

Specifically, remember to have a very focused agenda and assign a facilitator. Facilitators can be rotated to give everyone a chance to learn how to run a good meeting. It is remarkable how people respond to a well thought-out plan for a meeting. When a meeting is going well and team members are getting a lot out of it, the attitude that they are wasting a lot of "work time" seems to disappear. It is also helpful for the facilitator to ask for pertinent agenda ideas to customize the meeting to the team's needs. A week or so before a scheduled meeting, the facilitator might ask:

I am in the planning stages of our next team meeting, does anyone have anything to add to the agenda?

See Resource 6: Holding Effective Meetings

Tip 259. Set specific time lines and topics. Have an agenda ready prior to meeting time. Be specific with times for each item on the list. If teammates see that the meeting will run on a time schedule, this will help the attitude that the meeting is not a waste of time. In some teams, team members are not required to attend any meeting that they do not receive an agenda for in advance. As an announcement, say:

We do have a meeting scheduled today. It is planned to last two hours, with 15 minutes allowed for each topic listed on today's agenda.

See Resource 6: Holding Effective Meetings

Tip 260. End meetings on time. This allows people to plan to be the most productive with their time. It also serves as a reminder that this will be an efficient meeting. You might say:

Our meeting is scheduled to end at noon today.

If the meeting is done early, end it. Don't fill up the time with less important, nonagenda items.

Tip 261. Eliminate unnecessary or redundant meetings. List the meetings you have as a team on a chartpad and see if

you can combine or eliminate ones that have the same purpose. Don't ever have a meeting just to have a meeting.

  Category: Meetings
  Problem: Making Meetings Work

Tip 262.   Create an agenda and use a facilitator to lead each
meeting. This is a very important beginning step for an effective meeting. The meeting facilitator creates a list of the topics
to be discussed. It keeps the meeting on track and more focused. To help the team create the agenda, you might say:

  Let's list those items we need to talk about in our meeting
  today.

See Resource 6: Holding Effective Meetings

Tip 263.   Organize topics by priority of importance for your
meeting agenda. As a team, you will identify the most important items or issues to be discussed in your meeting. The next
step is to list them in order of priority on your agenda sheet for
the meeting. This will help the team use the meeting time most
effectively. An example of how you might begin this is:

  Now that we have the agenda identified, I see there are 15
  items we would like to discuss today. If you had to pick the
  top three in importance, which ones would they be?

See Resource 6: Holding Effective Meetings

Tip 264.   Go over the most important meeting issues early
in the meeting. It is best to address difficult and complex issues
when the team is fresh and can communicate clearly. The
facilitator or meeting leader might say:

  We have some difficult and important issues to begin with
  today, let's get started on those first things.

Tip 265.   Take notes and record decisions. Selecting a
scribe or note taker is an important part of any meeting. Keep
track of team decisions and action items. If you don't you may
find yourself forgetting decisions you have made and being
forced to spend time later making the decisions all over again.
A way to select a scribe might be to say:

We have need for a team member to take notes and record the key elements of our meeting. Sam did it last meeting, do we have a volunteer for today?

See Resource 6: Holding Effective Meetings

Tip 266. Have the right people in the meeting. Team meetings should have the participants who are involved in the topics and who are relevant to the discussion. This will help the meeting be efficient and there will not be a need to "catch people up" on what happened at the meeting, or to hold up a decision that needs to be made because the appropriate people are not present.

See Resource 6: Holding Effective Meetings

Tip 267. Summarize and debrief each meeting. It is very helpful to go over meeting "happenings" as the meetings conclude. It is helpful for each team member to review action items, decisions, future action items, and responsibilities. Every participant needs to know what outcomes were achieved and what is expected of them as members of the team. It is also a good time to discuss what made it a "good" meeting or a "not so good" meeting. A good summary might begin:

Thanks to everyone for a very successful meeting today. To end our agenda, let's go over our team decisions and actions items to be carried out.

See Resource 6: Holding Effective Meetings

Category: Meetings
Problem: Getting Off the Subject

Tip 268. Have a written agenda to focus the meeting. It works well to utilize a chartpad to have an agenda plainly posted in the meeting room. For some teams it is also a good idea to attach a time frame to the agenda items. When people tend to wander off-track, it is easy for the facilitator to point to the chartpad and show the item that is supposed to be discussed rather than dwell on how they got off track. The facilitator might say:

I see we are having a rather lively and interesting discussion, but I must point out by looking at our agenda that we should have been talking about item number four.

See Resource 6: Holding Effective Meetings

Tip 269.   Say something to get the meeting back on track during the meeting. Look for process problems (the way people are working together) and task problems (what is being accomplished). Things like having two discussions going on at one time, getting completely off the subject, or ignoring someone's input, can cause a meeting to be unsuccessful. Name the problem and call the team's attention to it. You might say:

I noticed that we are having a lot of side conversations about things that aren't on the agenda. Do we want to change the agenda or should we get back to talking about the new insurance rates?

See Resource 9: Facilitating Groups

Tip 270.   Keep a list going as the meeting progresses of other discussion ideas that come up outside the agenda. This idea is called *harvesting* and saves great ideas that aren't on the agenda so they can be discussed later. To keep the meeting progressing smoothly, the facilitator may have to table certain ideas or side discussions that come up during the meeting. Even though these discussions may be off the subject, they may be very important ideas. Be sure to harvest these future agenda items on a list for more discussion at another meeting. This keeps the idea and makes it easier for people to stop talking about it because they know it won't be forgotten. You might say:

I realize there have been a lot of great ideas we came up with today that I do not want to lose track of. They will be discussed at another meeting. I will jot down the list on a chartpad for future use.

See Resource 6: Holding Effective Meetings

Category: Meetings
Problem: Dominating

Tip 271.   Give the dominating team member honest, caring feedback. Sometimes people are not aware of how they affect others. An example of the kind of thing you might say is:

> Jim, I noticed that you spoke for 15 minutes of our 30-minute discussion period. Although I appreciate your opinions, it makes it difficult for me to express my opinions because there isn't enough time left.

See Resource 8: Giving and Receiving Feedback

Tip 272.   Establish meeting guidelines. These guidelines help to create team norms that will discourage dominating behavior. An example of the kind of statement your team might agree to is:

> Team meetings will not be dominated by any single individual.

Or:

> Everyone will be given an equal opportunity to participate in team meetings and influence team decisions.

Once the guidelines are agreed upon, when anyone dominates the discussion you can simply say something like:

> I think we are violating one of our meeting guidelines. Let's give everybody a chance to talk.

See Resource 2: Using Principles, Guidelines, and Boundaries

Tip 273.   Give the person something positive to do in the meeting. Sometimes people who dominate meetings are looking for recognition and leadership opportunities. Consider asking the team member if she would like a temporary assignment to fill one of the three roles in the meeting: facilitator, gatekeeper, or scribe.

See Resource 6: Holding Effective Meetings

Category: Meetings
Problem: Unmet Commitments

Tip 274.   Compile an "action item" list as the meeting progresses. When a meeting is actually going on, many ideas come up and team members volunteer to do various jobs that are discussed. It is a good idea to use a chartpad or board to record these items for future reference and as a reminder of who signed up to do what. By actually making a hand-out to those involved, it even becomes a better reminder to the individual who has committed to do the work. A way to use this in a meeting is to say something like:

> We seem to come up with some great ideas but we don't always act on them. I think listing them would be helpful to the group and to each team member. Unless somebody else wants to I'll volunteer to be the scribe for this meeting.

See Resource 6: Holding Effective Meetings

Tip 275. Be specific about time lines and deadlines with assignments and action items. It is good to track fellow team member's commitments, and a way to do this is by establishing a time when the commitment will be completed. An approach might be:

> Josie signed up to do this month's inventory. It will need to be complete by the third of the month so that we can make our inputs into the financial program. Will that work, Josie?

Tip 276. Follow up on commitments. Sometimes commitments aren't met because people know they won't be followed up on. Consequently, they fall to the bottom of the priority list. Post a commitment list. This is a checklist of what is being done when and by whom. By checking a recorded list, each team member can follow his or her own commitments. At the meeting the discussion could be something like:

> Let's take a look at who the team members were that committed to redo our compensation package and come back to the group with a proposal. I see it was Joan, Kim, and John. How is that project coming along?

Tip 277. Use natural consequences. If a team member isn't able to meet her commitment to get the compensation redesign project done, then she has to explain to the team why they have to wait another month for the new package. If the project she is working on is late and it causes a problem with a vendor, she has to talk to the vendor and make it right.

Tip 278. Create a work culture that expects commitments to be met. Every team member has a role in making sure commitments are completed. As you build your team and begin to relate to each other, the team should feel some responsibility toward one another for completing the projects each teammate takes on. It does affect the success of the team. Focus on consequences not blaming. A reminder might sound like:

> Rory, I noticed you were supposed to have completed the design for the new part. We really need to have this done as quickly as possible. If it slips one more week we will miss the product introduction schedule and cause a short shipment to XYZ—a big customer. Our whole team will look bad.

See Resource 2: Using Principles, Guidelines, and Boundaries
Resource 8: Giving and Receiving Feedback
Resource 16: Team Member Roles and Responsibilities

Category: Team Decision Making
Problem: Lack of Agreement

Tip 279. Focus on facts and data. Don't think about who is right, think about what is right. When team members disagree, sometimes it is because they approach the problem from a personal or emotional perspective. The best thing to do in a situation where this happens is to turn to data or facts on the subject. Use these facts to make smart decisions. An example of how this might be handled is:

> Jim and Elaine are still disagreeing and there is no way to resolve this thing until we have better information. Let's find out whether customers prefer the yellow packaging or the blue packaging by having a couple of customer panels come in and compare them. Then we can use what we learn from the customers to make the best decision.

Or:

> Instead of talking about how effective or ineffective we think the training was, let's ask the people who were trained. We could ask each of them to list what has changed on their team or what part of the training they have used since the session.

Tip 280. Use the "What is best for my team and for the business" approach when your team gets stuck. This is often the way to end disagreement discussions that go on and on during the decision-making process. By going back to the basis for any good decision, it often brings team members back to look at the decision a bit differently. What is best for the team should out weigh personal preferences. A way to refocus the group might be to say:

> We have heard a lot of great ideas to help us in this discussion about this decision. Let's just take a minute and ask ourselves, "which of these ideas is best for the team?" Maybe we can find a win-win decision in here, instead of one where somebody on the team has to lose something. We should agree on what makes the most sense for everyone.

Tip 281. Make a consensus decision. Sometimes the group cannot come to closure on a particular issue. Before you give up, try going through the steps for a consensus decision to solve the disagreement. A consensus decision is where the entire team makes a decision everyone can support even though it may not be the exact decision they were pushing for originally. It takes place after a lot of discussion has occurred, allowing all team members a chance to give an opinion on the subject. You might say:

> We have really spent some time hashing this agreement out. We should probably try to come to consensus at this time. Let's see if we can reach an agreement we can all feel okay with. Can everyone support including Tom's compromise wording on paragraph three of the contract even if it isn't necessarily your favorite choice? If everyone says "yes," we'll have a decision. If there are still people who can't support it, we will continue the discussion a little longer.

Try looking for some common ground you can build from (e.g., the team charter, a desire to help customers, and so on). If you are simply unable to come to a consensus decision, you might try voting (majority rules) as a last resort. You might also consider agreeing to disagree if agreement is impossible. At least that way you can preserve the team relationships even if you are deadlocked on this particular issue.

See Resource 3: Making Group Decisions

Category: Team Decision Making
Problem: Indecisive Teams

Tip 282. Brainstorm with your team. This is a great way to gather lots of ideas and information to help make decisions. By collecting as many spontaneous ideas as possible, the team can look at all of them and perhaps find something that sounds good to people.

Tip 283. Use an affinity diagram approach to help in the decision-making process. Sometimes teams are indecisive because they don't see a clear path forward. This can help. Give everyone small pieces of paper with adhesive or magnetic backs. Have them write their ideas down on the "stickies" and post them. People then read all the options that have been suggested and begin to rearrange them into groups of similar suggestions. When you have groups everyone agrees to, title the group of suggestions and have the team (or a subteam) write a short summary for each group. Everyone on the team can add his or her input to the list that is beginning to form. Soon it will become clear which ideas are most important in making this decision.

Tip 284. Use a priority voting method. Another good way to find the most important aspect of a decision is to create prioritized lists. The team chooses several options for the decision and lists them on a large chartpad. The team discusses the listed items to make sure everyone understands them. The facilitator explains that they will now prioritize the list. Each person is given a marker and is asked to select what they think is the best option. In cases where there are several similar items listed, the team member should choose the one that is worded best, or the team can eliminate obvious redundancies prior to voting. Each team member selects their favorite choice (or top 2 to 3 choices depending on the size of the list) and puts a mark by it. The facilitator then narrows the lists down to the few items with the most votes. If time allows, a discussion around the two lists would be good. After everyone has had a say in the discussion, then another vote may be in order. This will provide a conclusion to this discussion and a decision of the list with the most votes. For example you might say:

We have to figure out how to provide patient care during the heavy vacation period. From our list of 50 ideas we have voted on three top ideas: 10-hour rotating shifts, trade with the nurses in pediatrics, and hire temporaries to do the paperwork and free us up for exclusive patient coverage. Let's have some discussion on these three and then we'll decide what we are going to do.

Tip 285. Create a blame-free, risk-supportive environment. Sometimes teams are indecisive because they are afraid of making mistakes. Find out if this is true and have your team leaders and senior management help you create a work environment where people will feel more comfortable making decisions.

Category: Team Decision Making
Problem: Getting Information

Tip 286. Use a best practices study. When approaching a new business or team decision, it is very helpful to look at how other groups or companies handle the same type of work or decision. Often, by comparing how others handle a similar decision, it makes for a better discussion and idea exchange on the decision your team must make.

Tip 287. Create a list of your information needs and get help to obtain the data. Making good decisions requires good information. Have a consultant or someone else experienced with teams help you create a list of the necessary ongoing information and a list of some specific project required information for successful team decisions. Take these lists to people who can help you obtain the necessary data if you don't already know how to get it. Ask your team leader or other resources to help. Information about customers or finance, for example, may exist in current sales and accounting reports that could be made available to you. Other information may require creating new information systems.

Tip 288. Use a variety of information sources. When making a tough decision, it is best to feel like your team is equipped with all the data and information it can possibly handle. Seek inside and outside your company resources for information. It may be available from the finance organization, engineering, or from your own teammates. Learn from vendors and customers. Consider local university or technical school libraries. Look for areas in your company that can provide you with good information depending on your needs. Locating a team that recently had had to make a similar decision, for example, is a good idea. Find out what you can learn from them. Look at your own successes and failures. As a team, you could each be responsible for finding a particular source of information and sharing it with your teammates. You might say:

> We have a very tough business decision to make next week. How about if we check with the resources we talked about and bring their information back to our next team meeting?

Category: Decision Making
Problem: No Time to Solve Problems

Tip 289. Get help from management to obtain the necessary time. Prepare a presentation for management that shows a business justification for taking the time to solve problems. Make a specific, clear request for the time or additional resource you need based on your justification.

Tip 290. Reprioritize your commitments to make sure that your team is spending time only on the most important projects. Dump less important activities. If you find that you are not able to get rid of enough work to free you up for some problem-solving time, enlist the help of your team leaders and internal or external consultants to help you redesign the way the work is done to streamline it and make it more efficient. Pay particular attention to changing or eliminating those activities that do not add value from the point of view of the customer, such as time-consuming corporate red tape or other bureaucratic practices. Use this freed-up time from your improvements to do problem solving.

Category: Celebrations
Problem: Lack of Celebration

Tip 291. Have spontaneous recognition activities. When teams don't take the time to celebrate success, it begins to affect their work. When you do something great, celebrating is the best way for everyone to share in the joy of that accomplishment. Say:

> Our team achieved a new company record for the amount of tax returns completed in one month. Let's all have lunch together to celebrate our new record!

Tip 292. Immediate individual recognition can also be helpful, especially if this recognition is done with the team. To celebrate extra energy and good ideas, you might say:

> Gee, Martin, I noticed you created a great new process for handling customer calls. It saves our team a lot of time and improves quality. Our team should go out and celebrate your idea. What's something we could do with you or for you today to make you feel appreciated?

Be aware that inappropriate individual recognition can cause problems. Don't single out individuals for projects that lots of people have worked on. It makes the team wonder why they aren't also being recognized for their part on the project. Also be aware that in certain cultures, individual recognition can be embarrassing to team members.

Tip 293. Use diverse recognition. Don't get stuck in the rut of always using the same kind of celebrations and recognition. Try some different methods to keep the celebrations fresh. After setting up boundary conditions for cost and appropriateness, for example, have the team brainstorm different types of celebrations they would enjoy. Consider things like the following:

- Putting up congratulatory posters.
- Writing a news release and sending it to the radio station.
- Buying new office decorations.
- Buying new equipment.
- Having a pizza party.
- Distributing special shirts or caps.
- Having a baseball game.
- Have a dinner or picnic with families invited.
- Starting a team "wall-of-fame" and making plaques for accomplishments.
- Giving public recognition in sitewide meetings.
- Developing a presentation about your accomplishment and giving it to management and customers.

When a celebration is appropriate have a team member draw out one of the suggestions from a hat. Do whatever comes out.

Category: Celebrations
Problem: Positive Feedback

Tip 294. Give feedback as soon as possible after the event. Waiting to give the feedback loses the impact. Brief, genuine expressions are usually best. An example might be:

> Anthony, that was an exceptional job you did setting up that customer visit. It was appreciated by the entire team.

See Resource 8: Giving and Receiving Feedback

Tip 295. Give feedback to reinforce desirable behaviors. When positive feedback is given, it shows teams and team members that they are valued and their hard work is noticed. The desirable behaviors are likely to be repeated. Share feedback with team members, vendors, and customers. An example might be:

> John, our team appreciates your part in redesigning our packaging. We wanted to tell you just how much we like the new package and how we feel it is a great step forward for the entire company. Thank you for all your hard work.

See Resource 8: Giving and Receiving Feedback

Category: Celebrations
Problem: Keeping Teamwork Fun

Tip 296. Celebrate small successes not just big ones. By celebrating at small intervals, this helps the team build up speed and momentum for coping with the larger issues that may come up later. It keeps morale high, makes teamwork more fun, and creates an emotional reserve people can draw from later to tackle really hard situations. Find successes to celebrate. You might say things like:

> Fellow team members, we have reached a new quality accomplishment with less rejects this week than the previous two weeks. I bet next week will be even better. We're on a roll!

Tip 297. Create projects so that the positive feedback is built into the work itself. Sometimes the best feedback people can get is from the satisfaction of doing a job well. Seeing an important report completed, or a newly built wall that is perfectly square, or a happy client, a well patient, or a groundbreaking software code sequence finished is very satisfying.

Unfortunately, many jobs are split up so that people can't really tell if they have made progress on their work. In some cases, they may not even know how what they do affects the final product or service used by the customer. As much as possible, try to give people whole pieces of work, so they can get a sense of completion and satisfaction from their jobs.

Tip 298.   Schedule fun. Take time out of the regular work schedule to have fun together. Look at it as a kind of team-main-tenance activity. Just like you would take time out to maintain expensive pieces of equipment, schedule some time to main-tain your team. Whether you plan a special celebration, decide to go out to lunch together, or simply do your normal work together differently, take time to have fun with your team members. Have a dress-down day where people wear special, casual, or theme clothing. Start team meetings with a joke. Share your favorite cartoons with each other. Loosen up a little. One way to set these kinds of things up could be to say:

> Kelly has reserved Conference Room A for us this afternoon. Instead of our usual team meeting, lets take this time to find out more about our fellow team members and to celebrate some of our accomplishments so far this year.

Tip 299.   Plan and carry out "out-of-the-workplace" activi-ties. By leaving the plant, office, or facility where you work, the interactions between team members stay fresh and interest-ing. It creates a more relaxing atmosphere for people to get to know each other better. Try some team-building or training activities offsite. Vendor and customer visits or benchmarking visits can be fun and educational. It is often seen both as a reward and as an appropriate way to celebrate the positive things the team has accomplished.

Category: Team Design and Structures
Problem: When Teams Aren't the Answer

Tip 300.   Learn about alternatives to teams. Don't assume that everything must be done as a team. Study nonteam struc-tures that are used periodically even in team-based operations. Emergency situations, for example, usually require autocratic (one person) decisions to be made immediately. This person should be the best expert in the team to make the decisions quickly, and is not necessarily the team leader. In other situations a few people from the team may create a subteam to handle certain aspects of a project more efficiently than the whole team would. Trust is important in these situations. If your team doesn't trust people to do work in subteams, the trust level needs to be improved.

Tip 301. Don't use teams if they are not appropriate for you. Recognize that some organizations shouldn't go to a team-based operation in the first place. For example, if interdependency (working closely together) isn't required in your operation, or extremely high levels of technical complexity force most decisions to be made by individual experts, teams will add little value. This should be assessed prior to making any organization changes to teams.

Tip 302. Disband inappropriate teams. If teams have clearly been force fit into a situation where they are inappropriate they may need to be dissolved and replaced by nonteam operations. Be very sure this is necessary, however, since the process of disbanding teams is usually irreversible. If you later decide to use teams again, it will be difficult if not impossible, to put teams back with the same employee population.

Category: Team Design and Structures
Problem: Using Subteams

Tip 303. Involve your whole team in commissioning subteams. Normally these small teams of just a few people can take on decisions, problems, or work that would bog down your full team membership. Without learning about the value of subteams, trust in the subteam may erode. This can cause the full team to disregard your subteam's work and recommendations. The whole team should be included in the selection process for subteam membership as part of the team commission process.

See Resource 18: Selecting Team Members

Tip 304. Ensure frequent communication between the team and the subteam to keep people informed. This reduces the risk of problems later on. The commissioning process might include a schedule of updates. Have more updates for issues that are perceived as more critical.

Tip 305. Have your subteam create a purpose statement and project plan that can be approved by the whole team. This allows the whole team to buy off on what the subteam is doing and determine the success of the subteam after the work is completed.

See Resource 12: Planning for Action

Tip 306. Make sure that your subteams, project teams, and the rest, have clear "sunset dates" that will provide for the dissolving of the subteam after the task is completed. Without these project completion criteria it is difficult to dissolve the subteams. The natural tendency is to find more work to do. This usually is not the best allocation of your resources.

Tip 307. Have the subteam go through a similar set-up process as the full team does. Create a charter as suggested in Resource 1: Creating a Team Charter and operating guidelines as suggested in Resource 2: Using Principles, Guidelines, and Boundaries. Although this requires an up-front investment of a few hours, it will save you time and headaches in the long run.

See Resource 1: Creating a Team Charter
Resource 2: Using Principles, Guidelines, and Boundaries

    Category: Team Design and Structures
    Problem: Selecting Appropriate Teams

Tip 308. Learn about the different types of teams. There are several types of teams you will need to understand in order to use them appropriately. At minimum you should know that there are natural work teams (ongoing) and project teams (dissolved after the project is completed). Teams may require only a few hours a week or they may be the way your organization chooses to complete its work every day.

Tip 309. Create different types of teams for different activities. Make the differences clear for people by having different charters and operating guidelines for each team.

See Resource 1: Creating a Team Charter
Resource 2: Using Principles, Guidelines, and Boundaries

Tip 310. Go through a redesign process to ensure that you have selected the right kind of team for your application. Select a steering committee of senior management and employee leaders to oversee the process and commission a redesign team to analyze your current structure and effectiveness. Give the redesign team sufficient resources (e.g., time and budget) to do a good job. The redesign team should be composed of a true cross-representation of the workplace. This process should be redone from time-to-time in the spirit of continuous improvement.

Tip 311. Have a "future search conference" to include a wide number of the organization's population in a redesign process. Get good facilitation help to ensure that this process is successful.

Category: Team Design and Structures
Problem: Sizing Teams

Tip 312. If your team is too large, create subteams with distinct roles and responsibilities. Their goals should be directly related to the whole team goals, and membership should be rotated with some regularity to avoid people bonding more to the subteam than to the principle team.

See Resource 16: Team Member Roles and Responsibilities

Tip 313. If your team is too small to get the work done, combine the team with other teams for either the short-term (e.g., until the completion of a particular project) or for the long-term (e.g., a more "permanent" team structure with new ongoing responsibilities). If this is outside your boundary conditions, ask for help from your team leader to recommend this step to management. Put the new large team through a team-building process to get it started. At minimum, the team should establish a new charter and operating guidelines with all participants. Unless your new larger team has already worked effectively together previously, treat it as you would any new team that requires a very thorough start-up process.

See Resource 1: Creating a Team Charter
Resource 2: Using Principles, Guidelines, and Boundaries
Resource 16: Team Member Roles and Responsibilities
Resource 19: Team Leader Roles and Responsibilities

Tip 314. Use good business justifications to make changes. Changing team membership, whether reducing or enlarging the team, requires thoughtful consideration and good business justification. Make sure you have a good case before attempting to alter team membership. After you and your teammates have developed a good business justification (e.g., adding team members will improve the new product time to market by one month, or new members will save $100,000 a year in service quality, or new agents will reduce customer complaints by 300 per year, etc.), use a thoughtful design process to determine how people should be added or taken from the team. Get help from your team leader and the Human Resources representative to complete your process. Consider both business and personal requirements. Create a transition plan to ensure success.

See Resource 12: Planning for Action

> Category: Team Design and Structures
> Problem: Incorrect Membership

Tip 315. As a team, create a list of who should be on the team and why. Use this list as a discussion starter to get agreement on the right composition of the team. Make sure you have a solid business justification for any membership changes you feel should be made. Get help from your team leader and others to pursue your change ideas.

Tip 316. If changing your team membership requires screening and hiring new employees, remember to use good interviewing techniques and observe all laws appropriate to your area. Even if the potential team members are already employees of your company, you should use a good "on-boarding" process consistent with the information contained in Resource 16: Team Member Roles and Responsibilities, Resource 13: Team Communication Basics, and Resource 18: Selecting Team Members. After being selected, new team members should clearly understand their new roles and responsibilities and they should become oriented to the way your team communicates and functions. You might consider assigning new team members an experienced mentor for a time to help them become skilled in their new assignments.

See Resource 13: Team Communication Basics
Resource 16: Team Member Roles and Responsibilities
Resource 18: Selecting Team Members

Tip 317. Deal with performance problems before making any team membership changes. If the reason the team membership seems wrong is that a team member isn't performing, you should deal with this problem before changes are made. Never pass a performance problem to another team. Use the suggestions in Resource 15: Managing Team Conflict, Resource 14: Building a Collaborative Team Environment, and Resource 17: Managing Team Performance to resolve the situation.

See Resource 14: Building a Collaborative Team Environment
Resource 15: Managing Team Conflict
Resource 17: Managing Team Performance

Category: Team Design and Structures
Problem: Multiple Site Teams

Tip 318. Have regular teleconferences. One of the biggest problems with geographically dispersed teams is that communication is difficult. Set up a time for 15-minute morning teleconference meetings that are strictly observed.

Tip 319. Establish a virtual office location to serve as a home base for members of the team. This may be something as simple as a common electronic bulletin board, or mail box location, or something as substantive as a centrally located team room or team office with desks and chairs. Even if the team members only use the virtual office location occasionally, it will provide a psychological base for their operations.

Tip 320. An appropriate start-up procedure for these types of teams is critical. A face-to-face meeting of several days at the beginning of the project is a wise investment. Since you won't have the advantage of a common location and frequent face-to-face interaction to help keep you on track, a charter, operating guidelines, team project plans, and common team goals are essential. Follow the processes outlined in Resource 1: Creating a Team Charter, Resource 2: Using Principles, Guidelines, and Boundaries, Resource 7: Goal Setting and Measuring Results, and Resource 12: Planning for Action. Include specific agreements about how your team will make decisions, communicate, solve problems, and make clear responsibility assignments. Skimping on the internal infrastructure development of these types of teams can be disastrous. Provide appropriate translators for members of the team who do not share the most common language.

See Resource 1: Creating a Team Charter
Resource 2: Using Principles, Guidelines, and Boundaries
Resource 7: Goal Setting and Measuring Results
Resource 12: Planning for Action
Resource 17: Managing Team Performance

Category: Team Leader Problems
Problem: Not Walking the Talk

Note: Some of the ideas in this section about team leaders may be outside your team's boundary conditions or authority. Not all of them may be possible in your organization. Seek the help of your Human Resources organization and/or your sponsoring manager or other senior management sponsor in implementing any of these suggestions you are unsure about.

Tip 321.   Try giving gentle positive reinforcement when the team leader does the right thing.

Tip 322.   If this problem is affecting the work of you and the team, make an appointment with your Human Resource representative and ask for some advice on how to deal with it.

Tip 323.   Tell the team leader how you feel when she doesn't walk the talk. Be specific and focus on how this affects your work and the work of the team. Use the process suggested in Resource 8: Giving and Receiving Feedback to make your point and remember to offer suggestions about what the leader might do differently. You might say something like:

> Mary, last week you said that you would tell the general manager how our team felt about the new software training schedule. I just spoke with one of the other people who went to the meeting and asked them how your presentation went. He said that you never said anything about our team's

feelings. I really felt let down. We need you to represent our views to senior management. Without your help I don't think we will be able to get this thing fixed, and it is causing us to waste about a half hour every day until we can get the training scheduled properly. Could you meet with the General Manager in the next day or two? I know it would make a big difference.

See Resource 8: Giving and Receiving Feedback

Tip 324. Offer to help point out examples of the problem when they happen. Don't call the team leader a hypocrite or say things in anger that may cause him to get defensive. This tactic usually backfires and causes hurt feeling on all sides. Instead ask him if he is aware that he is perceived as saying one thing but doing another. If the team leader says that he didn't realize this was happening volunteer to help point out the inconsistencies at the time when they happen. You might say something like:

Carlos, you may not be aware of this, but I feel like you sometimes say one thing but do another. Last week, for example, you said we needed to start scheduling our vacations on the big calendar in the team room. Everybody but you put up their schedule by the deadline. When you don't do the things you say we are supposed to do it makes me feel like there is a double standard around here. Things like that make it hard for me to feel like we are really all on the same team. It makes me feel like you think team leaders should have some sort of special privileges like they did before we started doing these teams. If that is how you feel, it makes me not want to get very involved. If this is just a misunderstanding and you don't intend to do this, I would be happy to point out these inconsistencies when they happen. Would that be helpful?

See Resource 8: Giving and Receiving Feedback

Category: Team Leader Problems
Problem: Abdicating Responsibility

Tip 325. Let the team leader know how abdicating responsibility affects the team and the business. Using the skills mentioned in Resource 8: Giving and Receiving Feedback, give the team leader specific information about this problem and recommend some possible solutions. An example of how you might do this follows:

> Leroy, I believe you want to do the right thing and not be a traditional kick-butt, take-names autocrat. But I feel like you might have gone too far in the other direction. Last week, for example, when you told the team that it was up to us to make a decision about which computer to buy, we didn't know that there was a procurement process we had to go through, only three of us really knew anything about vendor choices, and we had no idea about how important it was that we get something that interfaced with the accounting system until it was almost too late. It was a frustrating experience. Next time we need you to give us more help. We want to find out about the boundary conditions up front. I'll make you a promise: If you will agree to give us some appropriate assistance, I'll agree to tell you when I'm in over my head.

See Resource 8: Giving and Receiving Feedback

Tip 326.   Find out if the team leader has been trained to be an effective team leader. Recommend that he or she consider attending a course that will help them understand their new role and learn the skills of using boundary conditions, being a coach, and being a leader to the team.

See Resource 19: Team Leader Roles and Responsibilities

Tip 327.   Suggest a modification in the leadership reward system. The problem may be that the team leader is not rewarded and held accountable for the right kind of leadership behavior. In these cases it is unlikely that changes will be made until the reward system for leaders is modified. Talk to your Human Resources representative or senior management sponsor. There may not be a lot you can do about this other than mention your concerns.

Tip 328.   If there is no improvement after repeated attempts to help the team leader, ask for help from your Human Resource representative.

Category: Team Leader Problems
Problem: Inability to Let Go

Tip 329. Suggest the team leader work with a team to create a delegation schedule. Develop a "hands-off" plan as part of this process which specifies when and under what circumstances specific tasks or responsibilities will be given to the team.

Tip 330. Give the team leader feedback about how this behavior affects you and the team. Be specific and use good feedback skills. Try something like:

> Bill, I appreciate your enthusiasm about our new product development project, but setting up additional review meetings for us and you prior to each regular critical path review with senior management will most likely delay product introduction by several weeks. We really need that time to do our design work. And it feels to me like this is something that is inconsistent with what you told us about how you wanted this team to function as a self-directed work team. It feels like you are looking over our shoulder. Could we figure out a different way to meet your needs?

See Resource 8: Giving and Receiving Feedback

Tip 331. Make a decision and responsibility matrix. In the spirit of continuous improvement and clarity suggest that the team leader work with the team to develop a list of decision-making responsibilities. To do this write all the major decisions that need to be made on an ongoing basis (e.g., staffing projects, vacation scheduling, hiring team members, setting goals, and so on) on the left side of a chartpad page. Across the top of the page list all the parties who might need to be involved in any of these decisions (e.g., team, team leader, Human Resources, senior management, union executives, and so forth). Draw a matrix. For each decision, determine the relative responsibility of each party and place one of the following symbols in the appropriate place:

- *P* stands for primary decision-making responsibility.
- *C* stands for needs to be consulted before the decision is made.
- *I* stands for needs to be informed about the decision.
- Leaving a blank means that this party doesn't need to be involved in this decision.

Review and modify the matrix over time as your team becomes more experienced and can handle additional responsibilities. Going through this discussion can often help the team
leader understand which decisions really belong to the team.
If he later violates the commitments made during this meeting, assume that he has a good reason, and remind him of this
discussion. Revise the matrix as necessary.

Tip 332. Ask for help from senior management. Sometimes the only way to help team leaders let go is to restructure
their jobs. This is most likely outside of your boundaries, but
you might suggest some alternatives to management for their
consideration.

- Some organizations increase the leader's span of control
  enough that they simply don't have time to get involved in
  the same way as traditional managers would. They don't
  have time. A less dramatic approach is to give the team
  leader responsibilities for additional projects that will wean
  her from over-managing the team.

- Other operations transfer the team leader to an area where
  they are not required to manage people. Examples might
  include special projects or individual contributor roles
  where their technical or business knowledge can be utilized
  effectively.

- If the situation becomes too much of a problem, it may need
  to be treated like any other performance problem. Senior
  management usually gives the team leader a warning that
  this behavior cannot be accepted in a team environment.
  Other additional steps, up to and including termination,
  need to be taken if this is not successful.

Category: Team Leader Problems
Problem: Authoritarians and Autocrats

Tip 333. Using good feedback skills, tell the team leader
how his behavior affects the team and the business. Be specific.
For example:

> Misha, when you changed the sales districts this morning
> without discussing it with the team first, I felt terrible. I like
> the way we have become a team here, and I felt like we really
> took a huge step backwards today. If I misunderstood, it

would help me feel better if you explained what happened. If I didn't misunderstand, I'd like to hold you to your promise to modify things that are too autocratic around here.

See Resource 8: Giving and Receiving Feedback

Tip 334.   Determine why the team leader feels that she must be authoritarian through a joint problem solving process like those discussed in Resource 10: Team Problem Solving and Resource 11: Tools for Problem Solving. Brainstorming or force-field analysis are especially good tools for this process. After the root cause is identified, take action to improve it. For example,

- If the root cause is that the team leader doesn't trust the team members, create an opportunity for the team and team leader to work on something that will demonstrate the abilities of the team.

- If the root cause is a lack of knowledge or skills, the team leader may want to get some training.

- If the root cause is that the team leader doesn't believe that she will be rewarded for stopping autocratic behavior, help her look good by getting better team performance.

- If the team leader doesn't believe the team process will work, suggest she visit a successful team site to see it for herself.

See Resource 10: Team Problem Solving
Resource 11: Tools for Problem Solving

Tip 335.   Develop a delegation schedule to help the team leader put a structure in place that will help him transfer appropriate responsibilities to the team over time. This schedule would include the specific tasks to be transferred, and it would provide a development plan for your team that will prepare you for your new assignments. This structure may make the team leader more comfortable with the transition process and allow him to ease off the autocratic behavior. New responsibilities for the team leader need to be included as the team assumes increased responsibilities. Without this, the planning process may only make the team leader fear that he will lose his job. This is normally accompanied by anxiety and stress that may make the team leader more autocratic.

Tip 336. If there is no improvement after repeated attempts to coach the team leader, it may need to be treated as a performance problem. This is most likely outside of your boundaries. Ask your Human Resources, union officers, or senior management for help. Ultimately senior management may decide that the team leader needs to be transferred to nonmanagement responsibilities. In certain extreme cases they may need to be terminated.

Category: Team Leader Problems
Problem: Lack of Leadership

Tip 337. Let the team leader know that when she neglects to make certain kinds of decisions it causes problems for the team. You might say something like:

> Mary, I appreciate that you let the team make most of the decisions around here. But there are some decisions that we really need you to make. As you know, our contract defines certain decisions as management decisions and unless it's changed through our regular bargaining process we are uncomfortable with some items. An example of this occurred yesterday when you asked Bill and me to take disciplinary action with Walt. I don't mind letting him know that I don't think he is carrying his part of the load around here, but I feel really uncomfortable about something like deciding to send him home without pay for a few days. I think you need to handle that. We aren't ready for that.

Tip 338. Clarify decision-making responsibilities. Divide a piece of paper into two columns. Have the team leader write down which decisions the team should be making in one column, and which decisions the team leader should be making in the other column. Recognize that this list may change over time as the team matures. Review the list with management and team members and modify it as necessary. Use the list as a way to clarify decision-making responsibilities and set appropriate expectations.

Tip 339. Make sure that this is a decision that the team leader should make. Sometimes team leaders don't make decisions because they believe it is best for the team to make them. Determine if the problem results from the team leader being reluctant to make decisions or if the team is reluctant to assume appropriate decision-making responsibilities. Help the reluctant party feel more comfortable about doing something risky. Create a supportive work environment for risk taking by doing things like rewarding people who have taken a thoughtful risk and have failed.

Category: Team Leader Problems
Problem: Management Mistakes

Tip 340. Use mistakes to send a message. Ironically, making mistakes may be the best way for team leaders to demonstrate to team members that it is okay to make mistakes as long as we learn from them. To do this, avoid the temptation to cover up the mistake. Team leaders need to talk openly about what they did, what they learned, and elicit suggestions from other team members about what to do now. This is a good pattern for any team member to follow, and is an example of modeling. See Resource 20: Being a Living Example. If you are the team leader you might say:

> I wanted to let you know that I made a mistake this morning. Instead of telling the boss that we would have the job done by next Friday, I told him that we would be done by this Friday. Even though I'm reluctant to go back and embarrass myself in front of Jack, I know we can't get the thing done that quickly. I'll leave right after the meeting and try to catch Jack before he gets home. In the future I'll check with the team before I give out completion dates. Is there anything else you think I should do?

Tip 341. Without embarrassing the team leader, give her feedback about the mistake as you would with anyone else. Use good feedback skills like those discussed in Resource 8: Giving and Receiving Feedback.

See Resource 8: Giving and Receiving Feedback

Category: Team Leader Problems
Problem: Lack of Management Skills

Tip 342.   Suggest training. If it is a skill problem, find a way to suggest some training. Several classroom training experiences are available to help team leaders learn the skills of team leaders including managing by principle rather than by policy and using boundary conditions. See resources that relate to the responsibilities and skills of team leadership. If you are not in a position to suggest this directly to the team leader, suggest it to the training coordinator or Human Resources representative.

See Resource 19: Team Leader Roles and Responsibilities
Resource 20: Being a Living Example
Resource 21: Barrier Busting

Tip 343.   Senior management may try appointing a mentor for the team leader. The team leader would work closely with the mentor for a period of time to learn the necessary management skills.

Tip 344.   Suggest that the team leader go on a benchmarking visit to other companies or to other places in the company to meet with successful team leaders and discuss how to apply new management skills.

Tip 345.   Ask Human Resources about establishing a management support group that meets regularly to discuss appropriate and inappropriate management behaviors.

Category: Team Leader Problems
Problem: Lack of Team Leadership Knowledge

Tip 346.   If the problem truly is a lack of knowledge, training for the team leader is a good idea. At a minimum, cover the new role and responsibilities for team leaders and review key skills included in Resources 19: Team Leader Roles and Responsibilities, 20: Being a Living Example, and 21: Barrier Busting.

See Resource 19: Team Leader Roles and Responsibilities
Resource 20: Being a Living Example
Resource 21: Barrier Busting

Tip 347.   If the team leader has already been trained, his boss should provide a coaching process for him. A formal process will require that the boss acts as an active sponsor to the team leader who needs help. This process should clarify expectations, identify resources for help, and end with a development plan. Most good development plans include periodic review meetings with the sponsor to assess progress. If the team leader will not or cannot manage teams effectively at the end of this process, appropriate action should be taken up to and including dismissal.

Tip 348. Sometimes the last resort is to transfer the team leader to a position where she doesn't work as a team leader. Senior management may either put that person in a traditional operation where traditional management skills can be used effectively or put her in an individual contributor position without direct reports where her technical or business skills can add value to the team operation. Be careful to find or develop positions without diminished status or responsibility.

Category: Team Leader Problems
Problem: Doesn't Handle Performance Issues

Tip 349. Make sure that you have a clear system for dealing with poor performance. If it isn't clear who should be dealing with performance problems, have a team meeting to decide. Write a list of problems that should be handled by the team leader and problems that should be handled by the team itself. Create a definite process for handling these problems that allows adequate time for the person with the performance problem to improve. Most organizations use a multitiered disciplinary process with lesser penalties for first offenses (e.g., verbal or written warnings) and greater penalties for repeat offenses (e.g., probation, days off without pay, and so on).

See Resource 17: Managing Team Performance

Tip 350. Ask the team leader if there is a reason that a particular performance issue is not being dealt with. It may be possible that there are circumstances that you don't know about or that the team leader is unaware that a problem exists. Be specific and tell the team leader what steps you have already taken to correct the problem. You might say something like:

Tomas, you may not be aware that Joe has been late for three days in a row. I have already mentioned to Joe that this has caused us a problem because without his daily reports in the morning coming in on time, the whole team has been held up from their programming work. Would you talk to him?

Category: Team Leader Problems
Problem: Not Using Input from Others

Tip 351. Tell the team leader how you feel when this occurs. It is possible that he or she doesn't realize how you feel when your input is not being used. Be specific. Say something like:

Jerry, last week you asked for some of our ideas about how to solve the problem with our printing vendors. Although I gave you two ideas, yesterday you did something completely different. When you ask for my opinions but then don't respond to them, it makes me feel as if you don't really care about what I'm saying. I feel like I don't want to give any more ideas. I know that not all of our ideas are going to be implemented, but I wish you could at least tell me why my input wasn't used.

Tip 352. Determine if you misunderstood the team leader's request. You might say:

Sally, I thought you asked for my input on the XYZ Project. Were you asking for some of my ideas or were you looking for a sounding board for some decisions you have already made about the project? I'm a little unclear about what you want.

Category: Team Leader Problems
Problem: Playing Favorites

Tip 353. Give the team leader the benefit of the doubt and assume that he has been playing favorites unintentionally. Ask them about specific circumstances like this:

Bill, I notice that this is the third project given to Betty in the last three months. I have been interested in each of those projects as well and I don't understand the process to get those assignments. Could you help me understand how it works?

Tip 354. Have the team leader clarify how the decisions under question are made. Ask for a specific process to be identified that gives everyone a fair opportunity to be involved appropriately. Avoid the temptation, however, to make hard and fast policies as these may create unwanted rigidity and bureaucracy later on.

Tip 355. If you suspect any kind of discrimination (age, sex, race, and so forth) is occurring, contact your senior management or Human Resources representatives immediately. Ask these individuals how to proceed.

Four

Problems Between Teams

Problems That Make It Difficult for Teams to Work Together Effectively

Category: Working with Other Teams
Problem: Avoiding Problems

Tip 356. Problems among teams can often be avoided by having interdependent teams engage in a dialogue where they openly share their needs and expectations of one another. A specific process to accomplish this could include the following:

- Two or more teams who are interdependent having a meeting.
- Each team makes a list of their needs/requests from the other team(s) present.
- Each team presents their list.
- After reviewing the needs they have presented, commitments are made as to which needs will be met. Those needs that cannot be met are also defined, along with an explana-

tion why (e.g., not within the team's current charter, not
enough resources).

- An open discussion ensues that all parties are clear what they
  can expect from one another.

- Follow-up meetings are regularly scheduled (usually every
  two to three months) for the teams to provide feedback on
  how well they are meeting their agreed to commitments.

Category: Working with Other Teams
Problem: Resolving Conflicts Between Teams

Tip 357. Conflicts between teams can have a highly negative affect on organization performance. Once a point of conflict or disagreement has been identified, immediately confront the issue. Use good feedback techniques as described in
Resource 8: Giving and Receiving Feedback.

See Resource 8: Giving and Receiving Feedback

Tip 358. If a conflict between two or more teams is causing
problems for the organization, consider using the process
described in Resource 15: Managing Team Conflict. By using
a step-by-step process that allows both parties to first acknowledge the nature of the conflict and then jointly work toward
resolving it, the likelihood of an effective resolution increases.

See Resource 15: Managing Team Conflict

Category: Working with Other Teams
Problem: Solving Problems with Other Teams

Tip 359. When two or more teams are jointly working
together to solve a problem, first reach agreement on the
problem-solving process that will be used. By having a thorough process defined up front, such as the one described in
Resource 10: Team Problem Solving, time and energy will be
saved.

See Resource 10: Team Problem Solving

Tip 360. Often, it doesn't make sense for the entire membership of two or more teams to meet to work on problems of
joint concern. In such instances, each team should send repre-

sentative members to the problem-solving meeting. Determine which members of the team have the necessary knowledge and expertise to help in the problem-solving discussions.

Tip 361.   In problem-solving meetings among teams, it is critical that good team meeting and facilitation practices are being utilized.

See Resource 6: Holding Effective Meetings
Resource 9: Facilitating Groups

Tip 362.   When a team is newly formed, even if it is a temporary team focused on solving a single issue, it is helpful for its membership to spend time clearly defining the purpose of the team. The process in Resource 1: Creating a Team Charter is helpful for assuring the team is clear about its purpose and highly focused.

See Resource 1: Creating a Team Charter

Five

Enterprisewide Problems

Problems That Can Hinder Teams Across the Entire Organization

Category: Corporate Management and Policies
Problem: Working with Senior Management

Tip 363. Don't be afraid to speak openly about your concerns with senior management. Sometimes senior management will start a change process and then not provide the support necessary to make it successful. Confronting senior management may seem frightening, but it can be done successfully and with a minimum of risk. It can even raise the level of respect and trust that senior management has in you and your team. Use good feedback skills and remember to stay focused on what is best for the business.

Tip 364. Make a presentation to management about your inability to accomplish your charter. If senior management isn't providing the resources (e.g., money, time, people, equipment, and so on) necessary for success, use your team leader or someone well placed with senior management to help you. At a team meeting, review your charter and boundary conditions to ensure that what you are asking for is within your scope. Next, develop a short presentation (informal is usually best) showing how the lack of those resources is clearly keeping your team from fulfilling its charter. Use your team leader to help you find opportunities to get your case heard. To senior management, you might say:

> Our team is feeling blocked and unable to fulfill our charter without some of the resources we need. We want to fix it and get on with our work. How would it be best for us to talk with you about this?

This lets them tell you how best to determine what's needed. Be polite, be clear, and be specific about what you need and how it will help you fulfill the charter that they have already agreed to.

See Resource 1: Creating a Team Charter
Resource 2: Principles, Guidelines, and Boundaries

Tip 365.   Give them feedback. If senior management is saying or doing things that hurt rather than help, it's always better to assume that they mean well and that they don't understand how their behavior comes across. This will help put you in the right frame of mind to help them. You might say:

> I know that you're really trying to make this process successful and I have some reactions to share with you if you're interested.

If they say "yes" (they almost always do), then describe what they said or did and how it came across. Talk about how it made you feel. Be specific. If that part goes well, you might also tell them what they might have said or done instead that may have worked better.

Once you've said your piece, then stop. Keep it simple and the tone positive and helpful. You may also say:

> As things like this come up, how would it be best to talk with you about them?

This lets them help plan how you could best provide effective feedback on an ongoing basis.

Tip 366.   Get your case heard about broken promises. If senior management isn't keeping its promises, review your charter and boundary conditions at a team meeting to ensure that you're doing what is within the scope of your team responsibilities. This will help avoid problems as you push to have promises kept.

Determine how promises not being kept are keeping you from fulfilling your charter. Get your team leader's help in framing your case and getting it heard. You might say to senior management:

> We've been promised some things that have yet to happen and that's keeping us from doing our job. We need to know if something has changed that we don't know about, and if and when these promises will be kept, so we can make better plans and do our job. Will you help us with this?

Tip 367. Assume they are still committed. Sometimes management gets busy doing other things and looks as if they have lost interest in the process. It's better to assume that they are still interested and treat them that way. It will keep you in the right frame of mind to help them. You might say:

> We know you want this whole process to be successful and you want us to stay interested in it and make it work. We don't want to get the wrong message or idea about what you want us to be doing, so we need some help understanding what we see. Will you help us with that? What we see is. . . (describe what you see that makes them look like they are not interested).

Share with them what you believe are key signs management is interested and why you think so. This may be a surprise to them. You and your team might also be surprised that how they show their interest is very different from what you are watching for.

Category: Corporate Management and Policies
Problem: Lack of Senior Management Support

Tip 368. Keep management informed. Many times team efforts start in the middle of the organization where people are trying to solve real problems. Those processes often get pretty far advanced before senior management has to become involved. Helping senior management to get "on board" means helping them understand and embrace what you have already been doing. It's natural and important work for teams to do.

Tip 369. Senior management may not understand the case for change. Share your team's case for change with them. You might suggest they do one for themselves by answering three questions:

1. Why do we need to change?
2. What will happen if we don't?
3. What's in it for all of us if we do?

Tip 370. Demonstrate how your team is helping to accomplish senior management goals. Senior management may not see how teams can help. Ask them the key question for working with senior management, "What do you want to have happen that isn't happening now?" This ensures you are talking about things that they think are important.

They may say things like "Quicker time to market of new products or services," or "Better quality or service to our customers," or "Reduced cost of services." You might say:

> Let me show you how our teams are moving us toward that goal now, and how working together better would move us toward that goal even faster.

Then tell them how you think better teamwork and leadership would help. Don't worry about being formal, speak from the heart and give examples from your own team's work.

Tip 371. Get senior management to see teams first-hand. It's hard to imagine how teams work without seeing them in action. You might suggest that senior management visit some other organizations that have implemented a team-based approach to help them learn first-hand what it's all about. These pictures are worth a thousand words. It also works to have some teams from other companies visit your site, but off-site tours are much more effective. Chances are one or more of your key suppliers or customers has a good team story to tell. You might suggest executives start there. If so, those visits are helpful in lots of ways. They can have their learning experience plus take the opportunity to strengthen relationships with important business partners. If senior managers go with your union executives or key labor leaders this can also serve as a team-building opportunity. Companies and teams love to talk about what they are doing and what they have learned so these visits are usually easy to set up. Be prepared for waiting to see some of the more popular spots, however. Some facilities have a three- to nine-month waiting list.

Tip 372. Invite management to hear about your accomplishments. Senior management may not understand what your team is supposed to do. Share your charter and boundary conditions. Describe your team's role in the larger process of which it is a part; who you see as your suppliers, who you see as your customers, and your key learnings and accomplishments so far. You might say:

> We'd like to share our team's charter with you and help you understand what we're all about. We think the more you know about us, the better our communication will be and the better we will be able to do our job. We would also benefit from your perspective on where we're headed as a team. Would you help us with that? Can we arrange a time for you to come and sit with us awhile where we work so we can show you what we're up to?

See Resource 1: Creating a Team Charter
Resource 2: Using Principles, Guidelines, and Boundaries

Tip 373. Suggest executive briefing or training sessions. Senior management might not seem to be on board because they don't understand what they are supposed to do or how to support the process. There are seven basic competencies for all leaders in a team environment, including senior management. They are Being a Leader, Living Example, Coach, Business Analyzer, Barrier Buster, Facilitator, and Customer Advocate. Encourage senior management to learn more about their role and to study the process of leadership in a team-based organization. Also consider sending brief articles to executives for their review. Reprints from respected business journals which discuss team accomplishments and stories about senior executives in those situations can be useful.

See Resource 19: Team Leader Roles and Responsibilities
Resource 20: Being a Living Example
Resource 21: Barrier Busting

Category: Corporate Management and Policies
Problem: Restrictive Corporate Policies and Bureaucratic
            Red Tape

Tip 374. Tell people what you need from them to be successful. Sometimes an individual or group at Corporate will block progress for the team by not participating with the teams or by not giving up control. They may not even know they are doing this unless you tell them. It's always better to assume they really do want to help and treat them that way. It will put you in the right mindset to work effectively with them. You might say:

> We're trying to get something done that requires your support and so far we haven't been able to get it. We'd like to share our charter and timelines with you and see if we can understand what we need to do to get your help in this matter. Can we set a time to do that with you?

You may want to ask your team leader to help "grease the skids" for you. If your attempts to get what you need from Corporate fail, ask your team leader to help you. Busting barriers for the team is one of the key management responsibilities. Don't be shy. Ask for their help when you need it.

See Resource 5: Working with Suppliers
Resource 21: Barrier Busting

Tip 375. Determine who has the power to change restrictive policies and meet with them. Sometimes the team is blocked by old policies or practices that haven't been changed yet. With the team, identify clearly how the old policy or practice is keeping your team from doing its job or from advancing to more effective levels of teamwork. Ask your team leader to help you identify ways to get your case heard by those capable of eliminating or suspending the policy or practice. Be specific about what your team needs to have happen to allow you to get your job done.

See Resource 21: Barrier Busting

Tip 376. Redesign restrictive practices and nonvalue adding red tape. Sometimes bureaucratic corporate systems keep a team from doing its job—change them. Part of a thorough redesign process is to reengineer the support systems that everyone uses. Ask your team leader for help in identifying who to talk to to get a redesign started.

You may wish to volunteer to be part of the redesign team. Until then get clear on the support or permission you need to work around blocks in the system that keep your team from getting its job done.

Category: Corporate Management and Policies
Problem: The "Old Boy Network"

Tip 377. Understand network power. Dealing with an informal network that has real power can be difficult. Historically, everyone's heard of the "old boy networks" that exist in some organizations and have the power to get things done or block them as they choose. Today we know that any group of people with similar backgrounds, or experience or education can form a tight group that has power to either block or advance team and change processes. It's probably not your team's job to eliminate such networks, even if you wanted to. But, there are three ways to deal with them: use them, fight them, or go around them.

Tip 378. To use the informal networks, first identify which ones exist in your organization. It might be people with many years of service, especially team leaders or engineers or marketing professionals or secretaries. You may wish to ask your team leader to help you identify them. Next, identify individuals in the network that may have the same ideas or need for change as your team does. If you assume people want to use their power for good it puts you in the right frame of mind to work with them effectively. To someone who is not yet using their power to help teams, you might say something like:

> We know you have a great deal of influence in the organization and we would like your council on something. Would you help us by giving us some ideas on how to get done what we want to get done?

By asking for people's council, they do not feel obligated to help you. But they often will go far beyond what you might expect. Ask for their ideas on how to get your idea implemented and how to get around potential blocks. Chances are, they will tell you how they can help you do it.

Tip 379. To go around an informal network is the safest bet. If you don't need to fight, don't. Brainstorm other ways to look at the issue. Look for ways to get your work done by avoiding the interference of individuals in the network. The more teams go around them and are successful, the more they lose power. Over time they may eventually cease to exist as a powerful block.

Tip 380.   To fight an informal network is a hard task. But if you can't use the network or go around it, you can take it on and sometimes win. Ask your team leader to help with this one. Make sure you are clear about how you or your team is being blocked and exactly what's needed for you to get your job done. Share this information and all the specific documentation you can get with your team leader. Look for ways to get your case heard up the formal management chain. When you've finally won, be gracious in victory, don't gloat. You are interested in getting your job done, not in making enemies. If you can't win, don't get discouraged. Take all setbacks as temporary and go on to the next thing.

Category: Corporate Management and Policies
Problem: Office Politics

Tip 381.   Openly discuss politics. The unsavory side of office politics, like vampires, often fade in the light of day. Sometimes the best thing to do is to talk openly about what looks like politics at work. You might say:

> It isn't clear to me what the process for getting promoted is. It almost seems like it is more who you know than what you know or what you have accomplished. If that is true, that's fine, but I want to understand the process. What are the criteria for selection? Who makes those decisions? Could someone explain it to me?

Tip 382.   Suggest a climate survey. Gather information about how people feel about the workplace. Do something with the data you collect. At a minimum, this information with a modest improvement plan needs to be shared with everyone who filled out a survey. Focus on improvements that minimize the harmful affects of office politics.

Tip 383.   Create a charter and operating guidelines as a team. You might include statements about honesty, openness, respect for everyone, and doing what is right for the customer. These kinds of actions will reduce the problems of politics and will set expectations for a more healthy and productive work environment. Perhaps as your team sets an example for others, they may also wish to stop perpetuating political and other inappropriate behaviors.

See Resource 1: Creating a Team Charter
Resource 2: Using Principles, Guidelines, and Boundaries
Resource 14: Building a Collaborative Team Environment

Category: Organized Labor and Management
Problem: Teams and Unions

Tip 384. Understand the mutual goals of teams and unions. There is nothing inherently "anti-union" in team-based work systems. In fact there are many consistencies between what unions have traditionally sought for their members and the goals of team-based work systems including:

- Fair treatment.
- Worker autonomy and say in how work is organized.
- Continual knowledge and skill development.
- Security of employment.
- Quality products and services.
- Employee dignity.

Many unions openly support teams and have played key roles in a variety of corporations. In pursuing a team-based organization, maintain the focus on the benefits in helping address the goals of management and the union. It can be helpful for union members to tour facilities and talk to union members that are working in team-based work systems.

Category: Organized Labor and Management
Problem: Respecting Contracts and Agreements

Tip 385. Respect the contract. The labor contract represents an agreement between the union and management about how the workplace will operate. The intent of the agreement, from the union perspective, is to protect workers from being unfairly exploited by management. For management, the contract articulates what it can expect from its workforce and provides a single point of contact, the union, for dealing with labor-related issues. It is important that both parties work within the parameters and spirit of the labor contract when initiating a team-based work system.

Tip 386.   Use the agreed on process and consider "compacts." It is possible, even likely, that both the union and management may find elements of the existing contract that are incompatible with moving toward a team-based work system. These discrepancies should be noted and addressed in future contract negotiations. Many organizations are also moving to "labor compacts"—shorter agreements to certain principles and values which substitute for numerous specific rules and regulations. Although these agreements require a high level of trust from both parties, they can offer desirable flexibility to everyone involved. They also commit people to a higher law. These kinds of agreements require ongoing collaborative relationships between partners, not adversaries.

Category: Organized Labor and Management
Problem: Changing Restrictive Past Practices on All Sides

Tip 387.   Management must assure the union that employee involvement is not a means to turn workers against unions. This can best be accomplished by assuring early and direct union involvement in the planning, transition, and ongoing renewal of the team-based system.

Tip 388.   An effective method to get movement toward a team-based system in situations where there have been a number of restrictive practices on both the union and management side, is to set some specific guidelines for the negotiations between union and management with regard to the team system:

- There will only be changes in areas by both parties.
- Either party can veto the new team-based practices after a pilot effort is attempted (both parties agree to give full implementation support to the pilot to give it an honest try).
- A point of no return is determined after which the changes become permanent (this keeps the changes from becoming bargaining chips for either labor or management later on).

Category: Organized Labor and Management
Problem: When the Union Isn't Involved Early Enough

Tip 389. It is very important when moving to a team-based work system to get union involvement early on in the process. Obviously the union is a key stakeholder in the transition and without union support the effort will not go far. Gain early support by inviting union representation during the early discussions of teams. During these early meetings it is useful to describe:

- The organization's case for change (i.e., why a team-based organization is necessary).

- A vision of how being team-based could serve as a substantial competitive advantage.

- An outline of a process for planning and transitioning the organization to a team-based system that includes meaningful union involvement at each step in the process.

Tip 390. If there was little or no union involvement early in the process it becomes critical to be very open and share all relevant information with them including:

- Why management wanted to introduce team-based work systems.

- Why the union was not involved in the early discussions.

- The key points, arguments, and notes from the previous management meetings.

- What the future role of the union could be in the process.

It is likely union members will feel slighted and their suspicions heightened by the fact they were not involved early in the transition process. Management must be completely open and direct with their communication—the perception something is being "held back" or "sugar coated" will hurt the chances for direct union involvement and support. The union must feel, despite management's failure to involve them early in the process, that they can still trust management and that they have an opportunity to fairly assess the potential advantages team-based work systems could provide for union members.

Category: Organized Labor and Management
Problem: When the Union Doesn't Support Teams

Tip 391. Understand the underlying distrust. If the union does not support the "team concept," it is likely union members are suspicious of the motivations management has in bringing teams into the organization. It is important for management to try to understand—from the union's perspective—how past behaviors and practices have led to feeling of distrust in management. Before a management initiated effort to utilize teams can go very far, management must recognize and appreciate union concerns and apprehensions. Once these concerns are understood, a dialogue can begin on how to overcome the lingering effects of past practices.

Tip 392. Jointly resolve concerns. Some unions have not supported teams because of concerns relating to:

- The impact teams could have on the labor contract and the union's bargaining position.
- The misuse of the "team" techniques to speed up the pace of work or to increase management control.
- Being given additional responsibilities without legitimate power.

It is important to understand the nature of union concerns and attempt to jointly (management and the union) address them. By working jointly in resolving concerns, management and the union are modeling a team-based system.

Category: Pay Concerns
Problem: Pay Conflicts

Tip 393. Determine what isn't working on your pay system. If people feel the pay system is unfair or is rewarding the wrong kind of behaviors among team members, it may be appropriate to bring the issue to the attention of senior management. In bringing the issue up, be clear about how the pay system is getting in the way. Describe the specific behaviors the current system is rewarding and how these are detrimental to the team's performance.

Tip 394. Change things under your control. Pay systems are typically very difficult to change without strong support from senior management or, in unionized facilities, without fundamental changes in the labor contract. It is important to recognize that some inconsistencies with the way pay is allocated and the way a team desires to perform its work may continue to exist for some time. As a team, identify where the inconsistencies exist and agree to actions that are within the team's influence and control to minimize their impact. Next identify informal rewards the team can put in place (e.g., acknowledgment for a job well done, time spent at each team meeting reviewing individual and team achievements) that will help strengthen team behavior.

Tip 395. If the company is in a position to redesign its pay system, the following process is a helpful one to follow:

- Determine what is to be reinforced.
- Develop a reward philosophy.
- Determine boundary conditions.
- Form a design team (usually consisting of representatives from across the organization) and initiate the effort.
- Facilitate the development of the new design.
- Check the new design for consistency with the reinforcement list, pay philosophy, and boundary conditions.
- Try the new system.
- Evaluate its effectiveness.
- Implement improvements.

Tip 396. Be clear about what pay can really do. Often people have unrealistic expectations of what changes to the pay system can do in improving organization performance. A pay system that people are generally dissatisfied with can be a barrier to team performance, but changing the pay system without corresponding changes to the way work is performed, the way roles are determined, the way information is shared may have little lasting impact on team performance. The source employee motivation is less linked to pay than it is to having a sense of ownership and say in how work is performed.

Tip 397. Don't change the pay until you change the work. Remember that pay is supposed to support the way the work is done. It is a reinforcer of whatever the organization truly values. Because of this, it is almost always best to wait to change the pay system until after you have designed your team-based organization. Some organizations try to create a new pay system prior to implementing teams, and most of them find that to be a mistake. Until you know how the work is going to be done, it is very difficult to anticipate the proper rewards. You may accidentally institutionalize pay practices that will be harmful to teamwork.

Category: Pay Concerns
Problem: Performance Appraisal Conflicts

Tip 398.   Determine what behaviors the current appraisal system rewards that are detrimental to the team's effectiveness. Often by changing the way performance is evaluated, the appraisal system can become more aligned with the behaviors the organization is trying to create. The process described in Resource 17: Managing Team Performance is helpful for creating performance evaluation processes that reinforce teamwork.

See Resource 17: Managing Team Performance

Tip 399.   Change things within your control. In most organizations the appraisal system is very difficult to change. It may even require the support of Corporate Human Resources and senior management. First determine what aspects of the current appraisal system your team can change. Focus on getting these improvements in place first using Resource 17: Managing Team Performance. Longer term, work with Corporate to get additional improvement to the system.

See Resource 17: Managing Team Performance

Six

Problems Outside of the Organization

Problems in the Team's External Environment

Category: External Issues
Problem: Lack of Customer Knowledge

Note: In some companies it is important to get a marketing or a sales employee involved in any meetings where customers are present. If you are unclear about your boundaries in the area of direct customer interaction, get some help from your team leader, marketing, or sales representatives.

Tip 400. Schedule a meeting with a representative from marketing or sales to give a presentation about customers. People from these organizations are usually eager to share their knowledge about customers and will welcome the opportunity to meet with your team. When setting up the meeting you might say:

> Our team would like to become more customer focused but we aren't even sure who our customers are. Would you mind attending one of our team meetings to tell us about

the customers you work with and how they use our products?

Tip 401.   Create a customer focus team within your team. Charter them to find out everything they can about your customers using the process outlined in Resource 4: Building Customer Relationships and have them report everything they learn back to the entire team.

See Resource 4: Building Customer Relationships

Tip 402.   Schedule a face-to-face meeting with a customer. Develop an agenda using Resource 6: Holding Effective Meetings to make sure you use your customer's time as effectively as possible and ask them to explain how they use your product or service, what they like and dislike about it and what additional features they would like to see added.

See Resource 6: Holding Effective Meetings

Category: External Issues
Problem: Partnering with Customers for Long-Term Success

Tip 403.   Meet the customer and share the team's desire to develop a long-term relationship. Then share your team's vision, charter, and long-term goals to let the customer know you have something that is of value to them. Prepare for the meeting using information you gathered when working with Resource 4: Building Customer Relationships.

See Resource 4: Building Customer Relationships

Category: External Issues
Problem: When Customer Needs Aren't Met

Tip 404.   Always ask your customers for feedback and use it when you get it. Remember the skills for receiving feedback mentioned in Resource 8: Giving and Receiving Feedback. After you take an order from a customer, for example, you might ask:

Is there anything about our product or service you would like to see improved?

See Resource 8: Giving and Receiving Feedback

Tip 405. List the current quality measures for your team's product. Ask if these are the right measures or if others should be added based on your understanding of the needs of your customers. Take the list to marketing and sales employees and ask them to do the same thing.

Category: External Issues
Problem: How to Solve Customer Problems

Tip 406. Listen intently to what the customer is telling you and repeat their concerns in your own words to show your concern and to make sure you understand their problem and how they would like it resolved. State explicitly what you will be doing to resolve their concerns and commit to a follow-up time (if you cannot resolve the problem immediately). Resource 13: Team Communication Basics provides tools for listening to understand. After the customer has shared their concern, you might say:

> If I understand correctly, you ordered 15 parts and only received 11. The four you did not receive are critical to a project you need to complete tomorrow and you would like us to have them at your site in the morning. I am very sorry about the inconvenience this has caused and will do everything I can to get you the parts you need in the morning. I'll call you in an hour and let you know what we will be doing to resolve this.

See Resource 13: Team Communication Basics

Tip 407. Do not waste time assigning blame or trying to figure out why the problem happened. Relay the nature of the problem to the rest of your team and focus the team's efforts on meeting the needs of the dissatisfied customer. Information the team has gathered from Resource 4: Building Customer Relationships will help the team take the right actions based on the wants and needs of your customers. An emergency meeting may begin like this:

> I just got off the phone with Todd from ABC Hospital. He did not receive four of the parts he ordered and he needs them tomorrow. Let's put our heads together and figure out how to make sure he gets what he needs.

See Resource 4: Building Customer Relationships

Tip 408. After the problem has been resolved schedule a team meeting to figure out why the customer did not get what they wanted. Use the problem-solving process outlined in Resource 10: Team Problem Solving and a tool from Resource 11: Tools for Problem Solving.

See Resource 10: Team Problem Solving
Resource 11: Tools for Problem Solving

   Category: External Issues
   Problem: Resolving Vendor Problems

Tip 409. Establish a solid working relationship with all the vendors to your team. Use the process outlined in Resource 5: Working with Suppliers to help you develop this strong foundation.

See Resource 5: Working with Suppliers

Tip 410. Meet with the vendor and explain the problem you are having. Be very specific about what the problem is and the required timeline for its resolution. You might start the meeting as follows:

> The last shipment of widgets we received was covered with grease. This is not acceptable and we would like to get it resolved by the end of this week.

Tip 411. Share the problem with the supplier and jointly use a problem-solving tool mentioned in Resource 11: Tools for Problem Solving. You could say:

> We want to continue the great relationship we have established. How about meeting and jointly working through a problem session to make sure this doesn't happen again?

Resource 11: Tools for Problem Solving

Tip 412. Stop working with the supplier and look for another. (Note: this is the least desirable option.)

   Category: External Issues
   Problem: Dealing with Regulatory Agencies

Tip 413. Refer all regulatory issues (employment laws, sanitation audits, financial reporting for tax purposes, and so on) to the appropriate internal resource. For instance: Your team may want to change the way it reports certain financial information that a team member knows has tax implications. You should approach the right person in your finance organization and say:

> The current reporting requirements for the XYZ process are very time consuming. Our team would like to change the way we do the reporting but we want to make sure you are getting all the tax information you need. How does this proposal we put together look to you?

Tip 414. Often, in their excitement to make progress, teams can find innovative solutions that have the potential to violate critical regulations. After you have completed brainstorming ideas, assign a team member to monitor the ideas for regulatory concerns. They might say:

> All of the ideas look okay to me except the proposal for shorter breaks but longer lunches. We need to bounce that idea off of someone from the Human Resources department.

If you have even the slightest concern that a decision your team is making will cause regulatory problems find an internal resource to review the idea.

Tip 415. Ask your team leader to provide education about possible regulations whenever they provide training on a new task. You could say:

> Marcia, we know we now have full responsibility for the cleanliness of our work area. Remember that list of regulations the Food and Drug Administration gave us after the inspection last year? Could you spend time in our next meeting covering the regulations we need to be aware of?

Tip 416. Discuss regulations on a regular basis, acknowledge that they can be difficult to deal with and commit your team to a team principle that states you will comply with government regulations. Resource 2: Using Principles, Guidelines, and Boundaries outlines a process for establishing and updating team principles.

See Resource 2: Using Principles, Guidelines, and Boundaries

Part Two

BFR Team Tools® and Procedures

Resource 1. Creating a Team Charter

A team charter provides a sense of purpose, as well as a clear definition of the team's role and expectations. Specifically, a well-defined charter will:

1 Clarify what the team is expected to do.
2. Focus the energies and activities of team members.
3. Provide a basis for setting goals and making decisions.
4. Help team members visualize their potential.
5. Communicate the team's purpose to others.

The charter should include the following elements:

Overall Purpose. The overall purpose should explain why the team is necessary and what basic need it is expected to fill. It may also include a description of how the team fits into the overall goals of the organization.

Key Customers. Key customers are those that will use the products or services provided by the team. In describing the key customers, it is also helpful to identify who the team will report to.

Key Result Areas. Key result areas define what the team is expected to accomplish. The key result areas may include measurable goals or objectives by which the team can plan and monitor their progress.

Guiding Principles. Guiding principles describe basic beliefs, values, or parameters by which the team will operate.

Time Frames. Time frames outline the time commitments required by the team. Time frames can include major deadlines, or number of hours necessary to accomplish team objectives.

The following steps are helpful when creating a charter for your team.

1. *Prepare your own thoughts and ideas.* Prior to meeting as a team, each team member should take time to think about each of the key elements that should be included in the team charter.

2. *Jointly brainstorm all thoughts and ideas.* As you meet as a team, it is essential that all team members have the chance to voice their feelings. By doing so, one team member may be able to build off another's ideas. Be sure to record all ideas on the board or chart paper and be careful not to evaluate the ideas yet.

3. *Develop a rough draft of the charter.* Once everyone has had a chance to voice their views, you can begin to sift through the ideas and put them into an initial draft. At this point it may be necessary to discuss and evaluate certain ideas. Don't worry about perfecting the words; concentrate more on gaining understanding and agreeing to the main concepts.

4. *Allow the draft to incubate for a few days.* Once the initial draft is created, it is extremely helpful to give everyone a typed copy to review and think about for a few days. Be sure to get feedback and direction from your leadership support and possibly from your key customers. Let the draft incubate before meeting again to finalize it.

5. *Finalize and distribute the charter.* After a few days of review and incubation, the team should meet again to finalize the charter. This may require some changes based on new insights and feedback. Once finalized, typed copies can be distributed to all team members and any others who might be interested in the information.

Resource 2. Using Principles, Guidelines, and Boundaries

Traditional management practices have emphasized managing by policy as a way to assure equity and fairness in the organization. Policies were the rules used to make decisions in areas as diverse as attendance, relocation, equipment acquisition, disciplinary actions, and safety. While some policies are essential, over reliance on policies can hurt team development. An alternative to managing exclusively by policy is managing by principle.

The following distinctions are useful:

1. *Policies:* Rules and procedures that define specific actions or behaviors.
2. *Principles:* Core beliefs that help people determine for themselves appropriate actions in given situations.

Examples of principles:

- We can accomplish more by working together than we can by working apart.
- We are more committed to decisions that we participate in making.
- Our goal is to know and serve our customer better than anyone else.
- All team members own the meeting and its results.

To effectively manage by principles, it is helpful to consider the following guidelines:

1. *Everyone should be clear what the guiding principles of the organization are.* The leadership team should be involved in communicating organizationwide principles, but your team

should also take time to identify and discuss key principles that are relevant to your group.

2. *Principles should be relevant to the tasks, decisions, and problems that the team is working on.* Your team's actions should be in line with your guiding principles. Some teams scrutinize all decisions against the guiding principles. Team members should regularly ask themselves, "Is that consistent with our principles?" Asking such questions on a regular basis helps to reinforce the team's commitment to their guiding principles.

3. *Clearly understood principles can help to weed-out unnecessary or inconsistent policies.* As noted earlier, the intent is to have formal policies and rules only where they are critical. Many organizations have developed such elaborate and often contradictory policies that the business would come to a complete standstill if all the policies were actually followed! As teams identify policies that are inconsistent with guiding principles, they should address the inconsistencies. Policies that are no longer needed to control employee behavior and that block productivity and innovation should be eliminated. Naturally, there are usually designated channels for dealing with policy changes. These channels should be used for addressing the inconsistencies identified by the team.

4. *Principles should be reviewed and updated over time.* While guiding principles should be written with the intent that they will be long-standing and enduring, they should also be periodically evaluated. Such things as wording changes to help clarify their meaning or the addition of new principles should be periodically considered. By revisiting the principles and looking at ways to upgrade them their relevance is further strengthened.

Operating Guidelines

Operating guidelines describe the behaviors team members agree to operate by and hold each other accountable for demonstrating during interactions with team members. Setting operating guidelines is important because:

- If the team does not deliberately set operating guidelines, then the team's norms (habits) become the guidelines by default.
- Operating guidelines foster trust and openness.

- They establish common expectations for team member behavior.
- They provide a common vision of how the team will operate.

The following steps are helpful in setting operating guidelines:

1. Make sure all team members understand what operating guidelines are and why they are important. You may want to review their purpose and discuss specifically how they will be used.
2. Brainstorm, as a team, a list of possible guidelines to follow. This allows everyone to voice their ideas and opinions.
3. Review the brainstorm list and agree on a final set of guidelines that everyone is committed to follow. You may want to combine like ideas and clarify others in order to obtain a workable set.
4. Refer to the guidelines often to help keep the team on track. This can be done by posting the guidelines on a chartpad where everyone can see them.
5. Periodically review the guidelines and make any necessary changes, additions, or deletions. For the guidelines to be effective, they must remain current and relevant to the needs of the team.

When writing operating guidelines, use terms that describe observable behaviors, not attitudes or feelings. Be sure to post the guidelines where they can be seen and referred to during team meetings and set aside time in each meeting to review how well the team is working (process check).

Boundary Conditions

Boundary conditions describe the constraints or limitations the team must consider when making a decision. Boundary conditions are usually established prior to a decision making session and help the team focus on a practical solution to the issue they face. Boundary conditions often include:

- Budget available
- Resources available
- Required time frame for implementation

- The "fit" with the overall organization strategy

Resource 3. Making Group Decisions

There are three challenges that must be met for an effective team decision to be made:

1. *It must be timely.* Most teams have "windows of opportunity" that quickly open and shut. Decisions often need to be made, and action taken, quickly.

2. *It must be of high quality.* In today's work environment, doing things right the first time can make all the difference in the world. In many cases there is no second chance. Therefore, decisions must be accurate, precise, and well thought out.

3. *It must foster commitment in others.* The most accurate decision in the world is of little value if no one is willing to support and implement the decision. This is the essence of commitment. Often, even a mediocre decision that is supported with commitment can produce greater results than a good decision without commitment.

Making Decisions

Organizations use a variety of methods for making decisions. The appropriateness of any one method depends on the situation in which the decision must be made. Some of the more common methods for making decisions include autocratic, democratic, consensus, and unanimous.

Autocratic. The decision is made by one individual or a small group of individuals. This individual is often the manager or supervisor "in charge."

Democratic. Voting is usually the way decision making is accomplished. In simple form, everyone gets a vote. The alternative with the most votes wins.

Consensus. Consensus decision making occurs when all team members are committed to support the decision. Consensus does not mean that everyone agrees the best possible decision has been reached, but it does mean everyone can support the decision and does not feel they are compromising their ethics, values, or interests in doing so.

Unanimous. Unanimous decision making means that everyone agrees the best possible decision has been made. This is different from consensus where some group members may feel the best decision has not been reached, but they do agree to support the decision.

Reaching Consensus as a Team

Consensus decision making is a method requiring the dedicated involvement of all team members. In reaching consensus, it is helpful for all team members to consider the following criteria:

- I've heard your position;
- I believe you have heard my position;
- The decision does not compromise my values and ethics;
- I can support the proposed decision.

Steps to Reaching Consensus

The following steps are helpful when reaching consensus as a team.

1. *Define the decision to be made as a team.* This can be accomplished by simply stating the purpose of the decision and alternatives available.

2. *Gather information.* This may require postponing the decision long enough to get the information needed to consider all angles.

3. *Prepare your own thoughts regarding the issue.* You should know how you feel on a given issue before discussing it as a team.

4. *Share your thoughts with your team.* Be sure that you express your thoughts and feelings with your team members.

5. *Listen to the views of others on the team.* Allow others to fully express their views and try to understand their perspective.

6. *Make a decision as a team.* Reaching consensus as a team requires that you concentrate on reaching a decision that

everyone can support and not one merely based on your own preferences.

7. *Implement and support the decision as a team.* Once made, everyone on the team must take ownership for the decision and do all they can to see that it is successfully implemented.

The following list is helpful to remember when trying to make a decision by consensus:

- Be prepared to discuss the issues.
- Do your homework and be prepared to explain your position.
- Stay focused on the purpose of the decision.
- Say what is on your mind and take responsibility for being heard.
- Listen so that you understand others.
- Consider differing opinions as helpful to making a quality decision.
- Avoid the urge to wrap things up too soon.
- Make sure that everyone has been heard and that all points have been considered.
- Don't be afraid to address conflict.
- Confront ideas and issues, not people.
- Work for a quality decision and not just your preferred choice.
- Agree to the final decision only if you feel you can support it.
- Be honest about what you think.

What you think and what you feel are important not only to the quality of a decision, but also to the quality of the implementation.

Times When Consensus May Not Be Appropriate

There are times when consensus is not appropriate or just not possible. Some examples of situations where consensus is not appropriate include the following:

- Your manager has indicated that the decision is not up for discussion. It is outside the boundary conditions of the team.
- There is a crisis situation where there is no time to reach consensus. Immediate action is required.
- The team does not have the technical expertise to make the decision.

It is important to point out that, although these examples are valid reasons for not attempting consensus, they are also often used as excuses for not trying.

Resource 4. Building Customer Relationships

There are four key steps to developing and maintaining strong customer relationships. They are:

1. Identifying your customers.
2. Gaining customer understanding.
3. Clarifying customer expectations.
4. Using customer feedback.

Identifying your customers involves figuring out who your team's primary customers are and what products or services they use. Your team's customers may be both internal and external. Knowing the difference can be essential to your team's success.

Gaining customer understanding involves getting to know your customers in detail—who they are, what they do, and what they need. It also involves making your customers more aware of your team and what it can provide.

Clarifying customer expectations involves finding out what exactly the customer requires in the product or service that your team is expected to provide.

Finally, using customer feedback involves actively seeking out the comments and feelings of your customers regarding your product or service and using that input to continuously improve what you do.

Discussing Expectations with Customers

There are some simple guidelines that can greatly enhance your team's ability to gain insightful information regarding your customer's expectations. Keep the following guidelines in mind when meeting with your customers to clarify expectations.

1. *Pair up when possible.* When discussing expectations with a customer it is helpful to go with another team member. Doing so should enable you to gather more information and insight from the meeting. It will also show the customer that you are serious and consider what they have to say as important. Finally, having a partner with you can help to ensure that all important points are covered.

2. *Ask good questions.* Customers have a tremendous amount of information to share. Your task is to gain access to that information. The best tools you have for gaining that information are the questions you ask. In most cases, it is helpful to ask open-ended questions—questions that cannot be answered by a simple "yes" or "no" response.

3. *Get to the specifics.* Customers often will describe what they want in very abstract terms. They might use expressions like "fast response," "high quality," or "courteous treatment." It is important that you develop an understanding of what these terms mean to the customer. You may also want to establish upper and lower limits of what is acceptable.

4. *Listen, listen, listen.* Your customers know what they want better than you do, so listen carefully to what they have to say. Remember, your goal is to find out what the customer expects. A good rule of thumb is to let the customer do about 80 percent of the talking. Your 20 percent should consist of asking questions and clarifying important points.

5. *Avoid getting defensive.* It is possible your customer will give you some negative feedback. A natural reaction would be to get defensive and make excuses. Try to avoid this. Remember, you want to know how the customer really feels. Feedback about what has gone wrong in the past can be very valuable to your team. If you feel an explanation is necessary, try to provide one in a way that shows your understanding of the problem and your desire to make things right.

6. *Summarize what you heard.* There is no better way to check your understanding than to summarize what you heard the customer say. When summarizing, attempt to use some of the

customer's expressions and descriptions to show your understanding. Emphasize key points. After the summary, ask the customer for feedback, "How did I do?" or "What would you add?"

7. *Do not over commit.* One big temptation when clarifying expectations with customers is to make promises that your team cannot deliver. Remember the old axiom, "It is better to under-promise and over-deliver." If you make promises to customers to make them feel better about your team, but then your team cannot follow through, you will have hurt their confidence and trust in you. It is better to commit to what is reasonable and then work hard as a team to exceed what you committed to.

8. *Report back to the customer.* Make sure that you let the customer know what you have done with the feedback and what has changed as a result.

Resource 5. Working with Suppliers

In order to get superior products and services to customers, we must have strong relationships with our suppliers and vendors. Ideally, this relationship is a kind of partnership where suppliers share a commitment to customer excellence.

In developing a strong supplier relationship the following steps are helpful:

1. *Identify suppliers.* A supplier can be defined as anyone who provides your team with a product or service. An external supplier is an outside person or company that provides you with a product or service. External suppliers are not an official part of your organization. An internal supplier, on the other hand, is a part of your organization. They are the individuals, teams, or departments that help you in some way to complete your work. Both internal and external suppliers must add value to your team and to the final product or service.

It is often helpful to draw a flowchart depicting which suppliers are internal and which are external.

2. *Define supplier requirements.* An important step in managing supplier relationships is to identify what it is we expect from the relationship. To establish the requirements you ex-

pect from your suppliers, first identify what your customer expects of your team.

Key considerations include:

- What does our customer need?
- When does our customer need it?
- How does our customer use it?
- What else is important to our customer?

As you are able to obtain specific and measurable information regarding what your customer requires from you, you will be able to specify what you require of your suppliers. To determine what will be expected of suppliers, it is helpful to consider the following questions:

- What products or services do we need from the supplier?
- What are the key requirements of each product or service?
- How can we measure the key requirements?

3. *Communicate expectations.* The following steps are helpful for communicating performance expectations with key suppliers:

- *Remind the supplier of your team's overall objectives.* This will help provide purpose and perspective to the performance requirements. It also will give the supplier a better understanding of how their product or service fits into the overall goals of your team.
- *State your expected performance requirements in measurable terms.* Making performance requirements measurable allows both parties to discuss expectations clearly and precisely. Making requirements measurable means that you include such things as dates, quantities, frequencies, ratings, and lead times.
- *Allow the supplier to offer input and advice.* Be sure that suppliers clearly communicate their capabilities. Allowing the supplier to describe competencies or their approach to given projects is critical.
- *Reach agreement on specific expectations of both parties.* Remember that helping your suppliers succeed is in your best

interest. Be sure you know what their needs, wants, and desires are. Restating all agreements helps to assure clear understanding.

- *Review and document all agreements and expectations.* Writing the agreements down will allow both parties to have the same information, not for the purpose of fixing blame, but for the purpose of mutual understanding.

- *Agree on a regular feedback and follow-up schedule.* Scheduling a follow-up meeting helps to legitimize the agreements reached. It also allows for ongoing feedback and continuous improvement.

4. *Monitor supplier performance.* Monitoring and measurement methods might include:

- Tracking charts kept by your team and/or by the supplier.

- Observe supplier operations.

- Assess supplier performance by periodically visiting the supplier site and observing their process.

- Review sessions with supplier.

- Team satisfaction ratings.

5. *Give feedback to suppliers.* To sustain an effective partnership, feedback needs to happen on a continuous basis. It is important to provide feedback that both recognizes accomplishments and clarifies areas that need improvement.

When giving feedback to suppliers, remember the following points and principles:

- Be sure to give the feedback to someone who can make a difference.

- The process for giving feedback should be established by both you and the supplier.

- There should be consistent face-to-face feedback sessions where issues can be discussed in detail and resolved.

- When necessary, feedback should include written documentation and measurable outcomes.

- Positive results should be recognized.

Resource 6. Holding Effective Meetings

To hold an effective meeting, three conditions need to be in place:

1. *When, why, and where to hold the meeting has been clearly defined.* For meetings to be effective, they must be held at the right times and for the right reasons. Team meetings are appropriate when

- You need to be more involved on a project.
- You need to solve a problem that requires various ideas and expertise.
- You need to make a decision that affects the entire team.
- You have work that must be completed as a team.

Team meetings are usually not appropriate when:

- One person has a conflict to resolve with one other person on the team.
- The purpose of the meeting is not well defined and there has been little preparation.
- You are meeting merely to maintain the tradition.
- The issue or decision does not affect the team.

Routine meetings can be helpful, but be careful not to fall into the "routine trap." Routine meetings are especially useful for reviewing ongoing work, managing commitment schedules, and sharing business information. They are also handy when the members of the team have very busy schedules and calling a meeting on short notice is near impossible.

Some pitfalls in setting routine meetings are that

- People begin to attend merely because it is on the calendar.
- People are more inclined to miss routine meetings than they are meetings scheduled for a specific need.
- Routine meetings often occur without much purpose or structure and, as a result, they can sometimes turn into group gripe sessions.

The meeting place is also an important consideration. While the work area is often convenient, it is not always conducive to meeting success because of distractions, noise, and lack of privacy. In preparing a place to meet, consider

- A location that is reasonably accessible to all.
- Adequate space and size.
- Appropriate seating arrangements.
- Access to appropriate equipment (e.g., overhead projector, charts, copier).
- Access to rest rooms.
- Privacy and elimination of distractions.

2. *Adequate preparation.* Meeting preparation involves four critical elements known as PATI. *PATI* stands for: Purpose, Agenda, Time, and Information.

A clearly defined purpose will help those involved make the connection between the meeting and the desired outcomes. An agenda describes the steps that will be taken to assure the meeting's purpose is met. In developing an agenda it is important to consider: What steps should we follow to assure the meeting's primary purpose will be achieved, and what is the appropriate order of steps to follow for this to be an efficient and effective meeting?

When considering time, remember these guidelines:

- Plan in a little bit of cushion in case some items take longer than expected.
- Plan meetings at times that are convenient for all participants.
- Plan meetings at times that do not conflict with productivity or peak working periods.
- Keep track of how long your meetings are running so that you can improve your accuracy in predicting future time requirements.
- Be sure to always start and stop your meetings on time.

The information needed for a given meeting might include important notes, previous minutes, proposals, drafts, memos, or individuals who have something important to share with the team.

All four elements—purpose, agenda, time, and information—should be recorded and circulated to meeting participants before the meeting. This assures the participants will have a chance to adequately prepare for the meeting.

3. *Conducting and participating effectively.* The effectiveness of any meeting is ultimately determined by the enthusiasm and participation of those attending. There are four key roles that help sustain meeting effectiveness.

Team Leader. The team leader leads the meeting and usually calls the meeting to order and manages the agenda. When leading a team meeting be sure to:

1. Welcome and set the tone—review operating guidelines.
2. Confirm that you have a scribe and a gatekeeper.
3. Review the meeting purpose, agenda, time, and information.
4. Manage the agenda (e.g., item, time, person responsible).
5. Encourage, clarify, and keep on track.
6. Review action items established during the meeting.
7. Establish a follow-up agenda if necessary.
8. Close the meeting on time or sooner if all agenda items are covered.
9. Take a few minutes to evaluate how well the meeting went.

Gatekeeper. The gatekeeper keeps everyone involved and participating in the meeting. This is typically done by focusing on how team members are communicating and the group dynamics that are occurring.

Scribe. The scribe takes notes for the team. This usually includes key decisions, ideas, action items, and assignments. Scribes should be careful to accurately write down what is said rather than their own, comments. Groups often find it helpful to record the team's notes on large chart paper and post them on the wall. This helps team members stay on track and focused.

Meeting Participant. Participating in a meeting requires effort. Certainly, the team leader plays a major role in the success of the meeting, but so does each participant. Participants are to:

- Come prepared.
- Encourage input from other participants.
- Help the person presenting or leading the discussion.
- Help keep the team on track.
- Listen to understand.
- Take responsibility for being understood.
- Take ownership of the decisions reached and actively support them.

Resource 7. Goal Setting and Measuring Results

Defining and measuring your team's performance involves the following steps:

1. *Define key result areas (KRAs).* Key result areas (KRAs) describe the general areas in which the team is expected to produce results. KRAs should be based on customer expectations.

When determining the KRAs for your team, consider the following points:

- Be sure to link your KRAs to what your customers expect of you.
- By focusing on results, your team can select more purposeful activities.
- Measuring activities can be helpful, but only if the team also measures key results.

2. *Identify benchmarks associated with each KRA.* The following steps are helpful when identifying benchmarks as a team:

- *Determine who are the best.* The first step to benchmarking involves identifying the teams, organizations, or companies that are truly stand-out performers. There are many sources to identify this information including:

  Your in-house quality organization

  Managers and other teams

  Professional/trade magazines and organizations

Professional quality organizations

Your customers or suppliers

- *Learn what the best do.* After identifying the best, examine how they do it. What processes do they use? What training have they received? How are they unique? What do they do that we don't? What do we do that they don't?
- *How do the best measure what they do?* Next, it is important to identify how the best measure their performance. What measures do they use? What information do they collect? How often do they collect and review it?

3. *Measure your current performance.* The gap between where your team is currently performing and the benchmark it has identified becomes the basis point for setting team goals and establishing continuous improvement objectives.

4. *Set goals.* Remember, goals should be set so that they are attainable, however, they should also cause your team to stretch and improve. Goals that are unrealistic are frustrating. Goals that are too easy do little to help with improvement.

When setting your team goals, make sure they meet the following criteria. Goals should:

- Include a clear, meaningful measurement.
- Describe specific action to be taken.
- Be written down.
- Include a completion date or time frame.
- Be challenging but attainable.

Finally, be ready to change or modify your goals as you go along. In today's changing world, you need to be flexible. What seemed reasonable yesterday may be obsolete today. That is the essence of continuous improvement. Review your goals often and expect them to change.

5. *Track and communicate results.* Measuring team performance is valuable only if the measurements are current and ongoing. Only then can the measurements be used as a source of information in making improvement decisions. Therefore, tracking and communicating team results is a very important step in the measurement process.

The following guidelines are helpful to remember when tracking your team's results:

- Keep the measurements simple to read and understand.
- The team should own the measurements.
- Tie measurements to KRAs.
- Measurement periods should be regular.
- Team members should do the tracking.
- Make the measurements visual and conspicuous.
- Do not let the measurement process become more important than actual performance.
- Make sure the measurements are meaningful and honest.

Resource 8. Giving and Receiving Feedback

Traditionally, we have viewed the coaching role as that of the supervisor, manager, or some other authority figure. Certainly, supervisors and managers need to provide coaching on an ongoing basis; but the coaching process does not end with them. Team members are also qualified to coach other team members for the following reasons:

- They may know more about the performance of other team members' than the supervisor.
- They have a clearer understanding of how a given mistake, problem, or issue, will impact others on the team.
- Coaching fellow team members fits the values and principles of a team-based workplace.

Preparation is a critical part of successful coaching. Some opportunities allow time to thoughtfully plan what to say and how to say it. Many coaching situations, however, are so spontaneous that quick action must be taken or the opportunity will be lost. Whether you have ten minutes or ten days to prepare, it is usually helpful to consider the purpose, timing, and place of the coaching opportunity.

Purpose.   Coaching opportunities usually have one of three purposes:

1. *Coaching to correct.* These are opportunities that require corrective action—something is wrong and must be fixed.
2. *Coaching to develop.* These situations represent opportunities to excel—we're doing well, but here is an opportunity to get even better.
3. *Coaching to reinforce.* These are opportunities to provide reinforcement for achieving desired results and behaviors.

Timing.   In general, coaching is most effective when it is as immediate as possible. There are exceptions, however. If, for instance, the person to be coached is upset and unlikely to be receptive to the feedback, immediate coaching may not have much of an impact. The following points are helpful to remember when determining the proper timing for coaching others:

- Will the person be receptive to my coaching?
- Do I have all the information I need?
- Is there still time for the person to act on my coaching?

Place.   When coaching to correct or develop, it is usually best done in private. By coaching in private you protect the esteem of the individual and the confidentiality of the situation. When coaching to reinforce, it is often helpful to do so in public. This demonstrates that positive behaviors are acknowledged and appreciated by teammates.

Guiding Principles to Giving Helpful Feedback

Realistically, you may find yourself in the middle of a feedback session before you've even had time to prepare. In such situations, it is helpful to keep these guiding principles in mind:

- Do not "stockpile" feedback.
- Take personal ownership for the feedback you give.
- Confront by focusing on the behavior or issue—not the person.
- Emphasize and reinforce positive behaviors.

- When giving feedback, be sure to listen to the other person's point of view.

Steps to Giving Feedback

The steps to giving helpful feedback are as follows:

1. *State the purpose of the feedback.* Relate the feedback to desired team results. This helps set the focus for the feedback. It also lets the other person know what your intentions are.

2. *Describe your observations and perceptions.* Be specific about behaviors, incidents, facts, or perceptions on which you base your point of view. Be brief and clear.

3. *Listen to the other person's views.* Getting the other person involved in the conversation makes the process easier for both parties and helps to avoid defensiveness.

4. *Jointly agree on action to be taken.* Think of this as a plan of action. Your willingness to help can make it more effective.

5. *Summarize your discussion and show appreciation.* Receiving feedback is just as hard as giving it. Let the other person know you appreciate their openness.

Receiving Feedback

In the team environment, feedback is a two-way process. An effective team member must not only be good at giving feedback, but must also be good at receiving it. Part of being a good coach is being able to receive feedback.

The following steps are helpful when receiving feedback:

1. *Listen with the intent to clearly understand the feedback.* Try to identify the major areas of performance that are being addressed. Allow the person to finish before adding your interpretation. Look at the discussion as an opportunity to gain information and insight.

2. *Ask clarifying questions or paraphrase.* Seek to clarify the feedback you are receiving. Ask questions to clear up any confusion. Jointly discuss specific situations or examples that illustrate the points being addressed. Identify specific impacts on the other person, the team and the business. Restate key points in your own words to make sure you understand.

3. *Share your own views on the situation.* Once you fully understand the feedback given, share how you feel. Provide information that may explain the behavior while being careful not to make excuses. Try to remain as objective as possible. Consider how you would view the situation from the other side of the conversation. Remember, the overall objective of coaching is to jointly improve performance of the team and its members.

4. *Jointly discuss and agree on possible ways to improve.* Offer your ideas on how improvements can be made. Listen to the ideas of the other person. Make commitments regarding specific steps you will take to ensure improvement. Express any needs you might have for assistance. Allow the other person to make appropriate commitments. Schedule a time to get together again and discuss how the action plan is working.

5. *Express appreciation.* Remember, it is much easier for a person to just keep quiet, avoid taking the risk, and not give any feedback at all. After all, giving feedback is not easy for most of us. Be sure to thank the person for helping you to more clearly see an important situation.

Resource 9. Facilitating Groups

Effective facilitation requires a certain level of trust—team members must feel their ideas will not be put down and that their comments will be taken seriously. In addition, team members want their time in meetings to be used efficiently and effectively. The facilitator can develop team rapport and meeting effectiveness by utilizing the following seven strategies:

1. *Practice prevention.* One of the best ways to avoid disruptions in team meetings is to take the extra time to prepare effectively. When preparing for meetings, remember the PATI method, which stands for purpose, agenda, time, and information.

2. *Focus on operating guidelines.* The operating guidelines serve as a constant reminder of what is acceptable and unaccept-

able group behavior. Often a facilitator can get a group refocused in a positive direction by simply asking the question, "How well are we adhering to our operating guidelines?"

3. *Appreciate differences.* The strength of any team often depends on the diversity of its members. By having diverse opinions, ideas, and skills, the team is better poised to make good decisions and build off each other's strengths. It is important, as the facilitator, to remind members that differences of opinion are natural, healthy, and helpful to the overall functioning of the team.

4. *Utilize process observations.* The idea behind process observations is that many of the group's problems are unrelated to the content of their meetings (e.g., the agenda, the tasks, the decisions) but relate directly to the process (e.g., relationships, communication, involvement). The facilitator can watch the group and attempt to identify which behaviors, dynamics, or other process issues are getting in the way of the team's progress. The team can then examine the issues and agree on ways to improve. Being able to effectively observe group process takes some practice, but can be very beneficial to the team.

5. *Focus on reinforcement.* Reinforcement means recognizing and acknowledging desired behaviors. The most effective way to increase the likelihood of desired behaviors is to reinforce them. Continually look for opportunities to give positive feedback and encouragement to fellow team members.

6. *Share responsibility for success.* The success of the team is everyone's responsibility. By simply asking well-timed questions (e.g., "How do you feel this meeting is going?" "Are we still on track?"), you begin to share the facilitation role with others. Doing so helps to increase the level of commitment to team success.

7. *Model the way.* The actions of the facilitator will be noticed by the rest of the team. If the facilitator conveys commitment, support, and encouragement, then the team will also convey those qualities. However, if the facilitator's style is dominating or disruptive, then that too will be reflected in the team.

Balancing Task and Relationship Behaviors

The effectiveness of a team is often determined by its ability to balance task and relationship oriented roles. If, for example, a team is overly concerned for task, then the relationships among team members will tend to breakdown. People may begin to describe team meetings as "never any fun" and find themselves "burning out." Conversely, being overly relationship oriented may create an environment that is fun, but not very productive.

To help assure this important balance is maintained, consider the following four steps:

1. *Recognize the ongoing need to improve team meeting effectiveness.* Working in a team environment requires a constant effort by all members to improve the effectiveness of team meetings and activities. In other words, the improvement process is continual.

2. *Be aware of the balance between task- and relationship-oriented behaviors.* Members of teams naturally take on certain roles or behaviors that are consistent with their own style and preferences. Being aware of what behaviors are being performed is essential to maintaining that proper balance. Do task-oriented behaviors dominate (e.g., initiator, evaluator)? Do relationship behaviors dominate (e.g., harmonizer, tension reducer)? Or is there a good balance?

3. *Determine where improvements can be made.* By assessing the balance of task and relationship on your team, you should be able to identify areas where improvements can be made. This may mean devoting more attention to task needs or spending more time to build healthy relationships.

4. *Jointly agree on a process for making improvements.* Finally, it is important that all team members agree on the actions to be taken to improve team effectiveness. This often requires that the team update or revise its operating guidelines.

Dealing with Dysfunctional Behavior

It is important to recognize that the responsibility for dealing with dysfunctional behavior belongs to all team members, not just the team leader or facilitator. Examples of dysfunctional behaviors include:

- Being overly aggressive.
- Deflating or puting down others on the team.
- Lashing out at others.
- Arguing unnecessarily, with the intent to hurt or diminish the ideas of others.
- Disagreeing without apparent reason.
- Distracting the team with irrelevant issues.
- Using team meetings to disclose personal feelings and incidents.
- Cracking jokes.
- Interrupting others.
- Rambling on about subjects of little relevance.
- Acting indifferent, maintaining silence.

The following five steps provide a process for dealing with such behaviors:

1. Identify the dysfunctional behavior.
2. Decide whether to address it as a team or one-on-one.
3. Describe the behavior that has been observed without attacking those involved.
4. Explain why/how it is disruptive to the team's progress.
5. Get a commitment from those involved to change the behavior in the future.

Resource 10. Team Problem Solving

For problem solving to work, people working in teams need a common process for sorting through problems and jointly creating practical and innovative solutions.

Step 1. Recognize the problem. The outcome of this step is a clear, concise problem statement. The problem statement helps assure all team members understand the situation and assures that a problem—and not a solution—has been defined.

To recognize the problem, the following three steps are helpful:

1. *Jointly agree that a problem exists.* Before anything else, the team must acknowledge that a problem exists. At this point it is not necessary to know exactly what the problem is, but simply that something is wrong.

2. *Describe the problem situation.* It is then helpful for the team to describe the current problem situation. This can be done by stating whatever facts are known at the time. These facts can include observations, statistics, events—even feelings. The team can also state assumptions, which are very helpful, as long as they are recognized as assumptions.

3. *Write a clear problem statement.* Once everyone has a common understanding of the problem, the team should write a concise problem statement. This is often the first step toward documenting the problem. The written problem statement will serve the team when determining root causes and generating possible solutions. It is also helpful in keeping the team focused.

Step 2. Determine root causes. Knowing the symptoms is important, but the symptoms do not tell the entire story. It is critical to define the root causes of the problem. By identifying the root causes, solutions often become simple and obvious.

The three steps to defining root causes are to

1. *Localize where the problem occurs.* To effectively study the problem, it is first necessary to find out where and when the problem occurs. By doing so the team can target its analysis and avoid wasting time in areas that are not affected. By localizing the problem you may find that it occurs only on morning shift and only to product A.

2. *Gather and study relevant information.* Relevant information includes anything that can shed light on the problem under analysis. This information can exist virtually anywhere. It can be contained in reports, memos, work orders, and production logs. It can be obtained by observing a given process, conducting measurements, keeping check lists, interviewing people, drawing diagrams, or creating flowcharts. It is critical to make sure that the information used is accurate. Be sure to check its validity and reliability.

3. *Jointly agree on root causes.* From the information you gather begin to form logical conclusions regarding the root causes of the problem. Be certain that all team members agree on the conclusions made. Gaining agreement on root causes lays the groundwork for developing possible solutions.

Step 3. Explore possible solutions. Once root causes have been defined, the team can begin to work on possible solutions. The three steps to exploring possible solutions are to:

1. *Focus on root causes.* The intent of this process is to create solutions that really work. Therefore, it is important to fully understand the underlying causes of the problem. Some teams, in fact, develop success criteria, which explains how the root causes will be dealt with if the solution is to be successful.

2. *Brainstorm ideas.* Having focused on the root causes, the team is ready to generate ideas. Brainstorming allows all team members to share their ideas, however crazy they might seem. During the brainstorming session, the team should be more concerned about the quantity of ideas than about the quality of ideas. Evaluation can occur once all ideas are listed.

3. *Organize ideas into alternative solutions.* Once the team has created a list of ideas, it is time to begin to organize that list into a set of possible alternatives. This is done by seeking further clarification and combining like ideas. It may also involve building on each other's ideas.

Step 4. Select a practical solution. When selecting a practical solution, it is important to remember to not only work for a quality solution, but also one that everyone is committed to support and carry out.
The three steps to selecting practical solutions are to:

1. *Define success criteria.* The first step to selecting a solution is to define your criteria for success. Success criteria should describe the desired outcomes of resolving the problem. In defining success criteria, it is helpful to consider two types: first, those criteria that must be met for the solution to be effective; and second, those criteria that would enhance the solution, but are not absolutely critical.

2. *Evaluate each idea.* The evaluation step allows the team to consider the relative merits of each alternative. In some cases it may be necessary to use analytical tools to evaluate options, in other cases the practical solution may be obvious. When evaluating possibilities, consider both how well the option addresses the root causes and how feasible it will be to implement.

3. *Agree on a practical solution.* When agreeing on a proposed solution, team members should have a chance to explain their positions and share their insights. Reaching consensus as a team is important because it provides the foundation for successful implementation of the solution.

Step 5. Implement solution. Very little will come from your solution unless people are willing to work to make the solution a reality.

The steps to implementing solutions include doing the following:

1. *Planning action steps.* Planning is an essential part of problem solving. When planning, it is essential to determine what needs to be done, who will do it, how it will be accomplished, and by when.

2. *Taking action.* Taking action means taking ownership for turning plans into desired results. When taking action it is important to follow through on what you have committed to do. Team members should remember to keep each other informed on actions they take.

3. *Evaluating progress.* Evaluation should be an ongoing process involving all team members. The key to evaluation is to determine whether the root causes of the problem have been eliminated. Evaluating progress may also involve measuring task accomplishment, reviewing process effectiveness, sharing lessons learned, and celebrating successes.

Resource 11. Tools for Problem Solving

The old adage, "If the only tool you have is a hammer, then everything you see looks like a nail," all too often applies to group problem-solving sessions. It is important that teams are well versed and skilled at using a variety of problem-solving tools. Among the most commonly used are:

Cause and Effect Diagrams

This tool is useful in examining a variety of cause and effect relationships associated with an issue, process, or problem. It is most effective in dealing with technical problems or issues.

The following steps are helpful when using cause and effect diagrams as a team:

1. *Clearly define the problem.* Once the team reaches agreement on the definition of the problem, write it down.
2. *Ask for likely causes of the problem.* This could be done through brainstorming or by facilitating a discussion.
3. *Reach agreement on major causes of the problem.* Gaining agreement at this point is essential to successful problem solving.

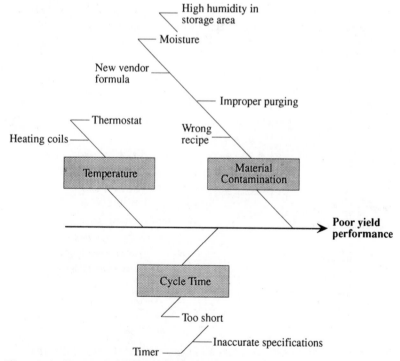

Figure 1: Cause and Effect Diagram

4. *Visually connect all causes back to the general problem.* Write down brief descriptions of each cause and draw lines to show their relationship. This is where the diagram begins to appear like a "fish bone."

5. *New lines are then drawn for new cause/effect relationships.* The further away we move from the center of the diagram the more detailed and specific the cause and effect relationships become.

6. *Analyze the diagram for underlying root causes.* By using this method, root causes often become clear. The root cause of the problem can then be addressed.

Variance Analysis

This tool is useful in systematically examining all the steps required to complete a project, build a product, or provide a service. The analysis helps to determine where variances are likely to occur and what their impact will be. By identifying where problems or variances are likely to occur, teams are able to redesign the work flow so that these problems can be eliminated or controlled at the point of occurrence.

Causes:

1. Wrong color paper pulled for order
2. Wrong weight of paper pulled for order
3. Wrong size paper
4. Paper arrives wrinkled
5. Folds inside out
6. Improper creases created during folding process
7. Wrong graphic design put on plane
8. Wrong graphic color put on wing
9. Graphics on 1/4" border of wing
10. Smeared or smudged graphics
11. Wrong message put on plane
12. Wrong spelling or typo
13. Message visible on exterior
14. Smeared or smudged
15. Does not fly 12 feet
16. Swirling motion in flight

Category	Matrix entries
Materials Delivery	1
Folding	4, 5
Graphics	3; 7; 4, 7, 8; 7
Writing	5; 11; 10, 13
Test	2, 3, 4, 6; 2, 3, 4, 6

Figure 2: Variance Analysis (This variance analysis example was developed based on the BFR Space Shuttle Shop exercise.)

The following steps are helpful when conducting a variance analysis as a team:

1. *List the sequence of steps in a given process.* List the specific steps, in sequence of their occurrence, for the process you are going to analyze. This can be done by starting at the beginning of the operation and asking team members to describe, in sequence, all the work activities that occur. Write down the sequence of steps on chart paper so that they can be seen by the entire team.

2. *List all variances that actually are occurring or could occur for each step.* Using the list of steps as a reference, list all possible variances. This provides a list of variances in sequence.

3. *Create a matrix.* Create a chart that lists all the variances across the top and all major sequences of the work flow down the side.

4. *Match listed variances to the steps where they occur.* Determine where the variances are occurring in the process and fill in the matrix. This gives a visual display of where the variances are occurring and the impact they are having on later steps of the process.

5. *Determine which variances have the biggest impact.* Based on the matrix results, determine which variances have the biggest impact to the overall process.

Pareto Analysis

This tool is useful for separating the few major factors from the trivial many. This helps in assuring those factors having the most impact are the first to be addressed. It is most commonly used when addressing quality, cost, or productivity-related issues. The tool is most beneficial when measurable data can easily be obtained. The tool is often used in combination with other tools.

The following steps are helpful for conducting a Pareto analysis as a team:

1. *Identify the issue to be analyzed.* A Pareto analysis works best where there is numerical data readily accessible. If the data is currently not available, the first step may involve gathering necessary data.

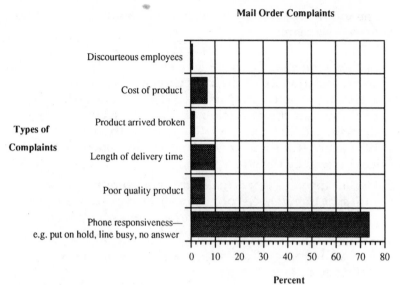

Figure 3: Pareto Analysis

2. *List all the elements that are having an impact.* This can be
   accomplished by looking at the available data or by brainstorming as a team.

3. *Determine which elements have the greatest impact.* In instances where there seems to be a fairly even distribution,
   where there is not an obvious 20 percent that is having 80
   percent of the impact, it helps to consider the natural groupings of the various elements under examination. By looking
   at these groupings, the important few often become obvious.

4. *Develop action plans to address the critical few.* Once you have
   identified the 20 percent that provide the majority of the
   impact, you can begin to take action to control it. In this way,
   the team is able to focus its energies on the areas that can
   make the biggest difference.

Force-Field Analysis

This tool is useful for identifying helping and hindering forces
impacting the team. The enables the team to visually analyze
the forces and isolate those hindering forces that are having
the biggest impact. The team can then focus its energies on
eliminating or minimizing the impact of these forces.

Issue: Add a new hire to the group to improve overall operational effectiveness

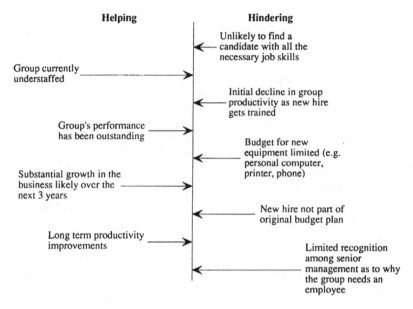

Figure 4: Force-Field Analysis

The following steps are helpful when conducting a force-field analysis as a team:

1. *Jointly agree on the desired outcome.* This should be a specific and clearly written statement describing the goal (e.g., "to develop a good working relationship with the marketing department").

2. *List the helping and hindering forces.* Draw a vertical line down the middle of the chart to divide it in half. On the left side list the helping forces. On the right list the hindering forces. To further illustrate the opposing forces, draw arrows from each item to the middle line with the length of each arrow depicting the relative strength of that particular force.

3. *Decide which hindering forces are strongest.* These forces should be the ones with the longest arrows. They represent the forces that are having the strongest negative impact on your team.

4. *Develop action plans to eliminate hindering forces.* Once you have identified the hindering forces with the strongest impact on your team, you can begin to develop action plans for eliminating or, at least, weakening these forces.

Stop, Start, Continue Exercise

This tool is useful for helping individuals give and receive feedback related to team effectiveness. The tool is most beneficial in dealing with conflict, interpersonal issues, and performance problems.

The following steps are helpful when conducting the stop, start, continue exercise as a team:

1. *Review team principles for giving and receiving feedback.* Being able to give and receive helpful feedback is an important part of this exercise. The team should review principles and techniques to giving and receiving feedback.

2. *Complete the stop, start, continue sheets.* Each individual should complete a stop, start, continue sheet for every other team member answering the following three questions: (1) What does this person currently do that I would like to see stopped? (2) What would I like this person to start doing in the future? (3) What is this person currently doing that I would like to see continued?

3. *Share the stop, start, continue sheets.* Once the sheets are complete, they should be shared with the person for whom they were filled out. This can be done by having people pair up one-on-one. After the first set has given feedback to one another, members rotate so they match up with another team member. This continues until everyone in the group has had the chance to give feedback to everyone else in the group.

Stop	Start	Continue
Checking up on me so much	Feel you're not comfortable sharing problems/issues you're facing—let's start sharing them with others	Being supportive of me and helping me bring issues before the group
Interrupting me during discussions		Your honest, caring feedback
	Try and delegate more responsibilities	Providing me with challenging work assignments

Figure 5: Stop, Start, Continue Exercise

4. *Develop action plans.* It is helpful at this point to have all team members describe what they feel about the feedback they received and what they plan to do as a result of it. This tool should only be used in instances where team members have full knowledge of each step of the process and voluntarily participate.

Weighted Criteria Worksheet

The weighted criteria worksheet is useful when selecting a practical solution from a number of options. This tool allows you to use criteria (weighted according to importance) to evaluate and compare the effectiveness of alternatives.

The following steps are helpful when using the weighted criteria worksheet:

1. *List and weight your criteria.* List one criterion in each of the spaces marked criteria. These criteria should describe the objectives you desire. Using a 10-point scale, assign a weight to each criterion to indicate its importance (1 = least important, 10 = most important). Record the corresponding weight in the spaces marked weight.

2. *List your options.* List the options your team has identified in the space marked alternatives. These alternatives represent the choices available to your team.

3. *Assess each alternative against the weighted criteria.* Ask the question, "How well does this alternative satisfy this criterion?" If it satisfies it completely, give it a 10. If it doesn't satisfy it at all, give it a 0. Otherwise, give a score between 1 and 9, depending on how well it satisfies the criterion. Place your score in the upper half of the appropriate box. Complete this process for each option against each criterion.

4. *Multiply each score against the criterion weight.* This gives you a weighted score. Place the weighted score in the lower half of each box.

5. *Add up the weighted scores for each alternative.* This gives you a total weighted score. The higher the score, the closer that option comes to meeting the success criteria you have identified. This worksheet provides you with objective data for making a decision. But remember, the decision is still the team's to make. Don't let the data decide for you. Use the data only as a tool.

Alternatives

Reducing Breakdowns

Criteria	Weight	A Higher grade oil	B Train employees	C Buy new fleet	D Preventive maintenance	E Do nothing
1 Cost effectiveness	9	9 / 81	6 / 54	2 / 18	7 / 63	8 / 72
2 Stress reduction	5	4 / 20	3 / 15	9 / 45	6 / 30	2 / 10
3 Decreased overtime	6	5 / 30	4 / 24	8 / 48	7 / 42	2 / 12
4 Decreased crisis situations	7	5 / 35	6 / 42	7 / 49	9 / 63	2 / 14
5 Increased customer satisfaction	10	5 / 50	2 / 20	10 / 100	8 / 80	3 / 30
6 Long-term prevention	8	4 / 32	5 / 40	5 / 40	8 / 64	2 / 16
7 Management satisfaction	7	7 / 49	6 / 42	1 / 7	7 / 49	5 / 35
TOTAL SCORE		297	237	307	391	189

Figure 6: Weighted Criteria Worksheet

Resource 12. Planning for Action

Planning is an essential part of almost every aspect of a team's work. The steps for planning team projects are as follows:

Step 1: Plan action to be taken. Action plans provide the team with a clear road map for accomplishing a specific project.

Planning specific action steps should answer these questions:

- What major steps are involved?
- What specific tasks are required for each major step?
- In what sequence should each task occur?

To answer these questions, a team should first determine the major steps in the project, then sequence specific activities required to finish them.

Step 2: Plan who will do what. Accountability is essential to completing projects as a team. Clarifying accountability can be as simple as asking for volunteers to be responsible for certain tasks in the project. When clarifying accountability for each action item be sure to consider the following questions:

- Who's responsible for getting it done?
- Who else will be involved?
- Who needs to be kept informed?
- Who will help make decisions?

Step 3: Plan for necessary resources. Overlooking resource requirements can cause unnecessary delays or disappointments. Planning for action should also involve a thorough assessment of what resources will be required. This step is often overlooked which can cause unnecessary delays or disappointments later on.

Resource requirements can come in the following forms:

- People—Who will we need for each step of the project?
- Time—How much time will be required?
- Materials—What materials will be necessary?
- Budget—What money will we need?
- Outside services—What outside help will we need?
- Equipment—What equipment will we need?
- Support—What political and practical help will we need?

Step 4: Take action. Taking action means turning the plan into desired results. Plans are of little value unless specific actions are taken. This requires that all team members work to assure progress.

Step 5: Evaluate progress. The final step in the action planning process involves evaluating how well the team is able to accomplish its plan. Evaluation is a key component of effective planning because it helps the team make necessary adjustments along the way and enables the team to improve the process for next time.

Resource 13. Team Communication Basics

Effective team communication is not automatic, it usually begins by learning common skills and basic techniques. In a team-based workplace, open communication is critical. Some of the features of open communication include:

- Aiming interaction at solving problems and achieving team goals.
- Team members trusting each other.
- Team members sharing a common purpose.
- Communication resulting in common understanding of ideas, feelings, situations, and expectations.
- Members encouraging and soliciting input from others.
- Inviting and dealing with disagreement as a vital part of making sound decisions.
- Sharing responsibility for communicating effectively with team members.

Communicating with Others

Keep these helpful guidelines in mind as you communicate with others.

1. *State the purpose of your message.*
2. *Communicate your message.* The following three components can help you communicate your message effectively:

   Main point—Describe your idea, opinion, observation, concern, and the like.

   Feelings—Describe how you feel about the situation.

   Effect—Explain what you feel will be the effect of this situation on the team (e.g., goals, cohesiveness, safety).

3. *Listen to the response of others.* This can be done by:
   Applying good listening skills.

Asking questions—Questions can help you clarify and understand the response you receive from others.

4. *Clear up any misunderstanding.* You may need to communicate your message again to ensure true meaning is conveyed. This can be done by:

Restating your purpose—Go back to step one and use different words to describe your purpose for communicating.

Restating the message—Use different words to make your point, describe your feelings, and explain the effect.

Adding meaning—Provide examples and experiences to enhance their understanding of your message.

5. *Summarize and move to action.* This step often requires the following three actions:

Review—Go over what has been discussed and understood.

Action plan—Initiate any action steps that are needed as a result of your discussion.

Follow-up—Set a time to resume your discussion.

Listening to Understand Others

When listening to understand others, keep these helpful guidelines in mind:

1. Listen for more than just the words, listen for meaning.
2. Remember that understanding the message does not mean that you must agree with the message.
3. If you do not understand the message, seek to clarify what is being said before you attempt to respond.
4. Work to apply appropriate listening skills when receiving a message.
5. Work to avoid the roadblocks to effective listening when receiving a message.
6. At the end of any conversation, take a moment to evaluate how well you listened for understanding.

The following listening skills are very helpful in improving communication among team members:

- *Paraphrasing.* Stating back what you heard but using different words. This is intended to verify meaning in ideas and opinions.

- *Perception checking.* Recognizing the feelings that you perceive in the other person.

- *Inviting.* Encouraging the other person to open up and tell you more. Indicating that you are interested in knowing more.

- *Relating.* Showing empathy for the other person. Make the effort to feel what they feel.

- *Acknowledging.* Using short gestures or words to indicate that you follow what they are saying and want them to continue.

- *Passive listening.* Just keeping quite and letting the other person talk.

- *Summarizing.* Bringing closure to a conversation by reviewing main points, agreements, and action steps.

Resource 14. Building a Collaborative Team Environment

In many ways, a collaborative team environment serves as the foundation for so many other aspects of team success. There are six components that are critical to creating a collaborative team:

1. *Common purpose*—All team members share and are committed to a mission that provides focus and direction.

2. *Trust*—Team members believe in each other, work for each other's success, and know that they can count on each other.

3. *Clear roles*—Team members know what is expected of them and how they can best contribute to team success.

4. *Open communication*—Team members continually share information, ideas, concerns, ideas, skills, and knowledge.

5. *Diversity*—Team members recognize and value their differences in styles, ideas, cultures, backgrounds, and expertise.

6. *Balance of task and relationship*—Team members work to balance the need to get work done with the need to maintain strong and healthy relationships.

Common Purpose

Teams that excel have a shared sense of purpose. Teams that flounder consistently attribute their troubles to an unclear purpose and ambiguous goals.

Tips for establishing a common purpose include:

- *Creating and/or reviewing your team's charter.* A team charter documents the agreed-upon purpose of the team's existence, but the process of formulating the charter is where the team is able to internalize the purpose.

- *Discussing why your team exists.* Regularly ask yourself, "Who are our customers? What do they expect from us? How can we best contribute to the success of our organization?"

- *Allowing each team member to express commitment.* Team members should personally voice their commitment to the team's purpose, priorities, and parameters. If they are not committed, they should have the opportunity to express concerns regarding the direction in which the team is headed.

- *Creating mottoes, symbols, awards, or posters.* These items can help to remind team members of their agreed-upon common purpose.

- *Using the common purpose to prioritize team actions.* Test all decisions, projects, goals, and plans to make sure they are consistent with your team's purpose.

Trust

Trust is a crucial component of a collaborative team environment. Trust is often slow to develop and easy to lose. In the team setting, trust requires the effort of all team members. To be trusted, you must be willing to trust others.

The following tips will be helpful for building and sustaining trust on your team:

- *Be honest.* The first step to gaining trust is to ensure that you deserve it. Be honest about what's on your mind. Live up to your commitments to each other. Do what you say you will do.

- *Work to eliminate conflicts of interests.* Conflicts of interest include any situation where the best interest of any team member is not consistent with that of the team or its other members. An example of this is an incentive plan that rewards individual performance so heavily that it undermines teamwork and collaboration.

- *Avoid talking behind each other's back.* Encourage your team members to do the same. When backbiting is tolerated, even those who are doing the backbiting lose trust in each other.

- *Trust your teammates.* Trust is a two-way process. Remember that the best way to earn trust is to trust others.

- *Give team members the benefit of a doubt.* Part of trusting your teammates means realizing that they are not perfect and that they will make mistakes. In times of doubt, give them your support and show them that you are genuinely interested in their success.

Clear Roles

Confusion over team member roles and expectations is a leading cause of frustration and tension in the team setting. That confusion can quickly lead to other problems such as distrust, lack of communication, and hidden agendas. People's false assumptions about who will do what can quickly lead to important tasks falling through the cracks.

The following tips will be helpful for maintaining clear roles and expectations on your team:

Review team member roles frequently. Set time aside in team meetings to review individual responsibilities. Use something like the following role model to start your discussion. Fill in

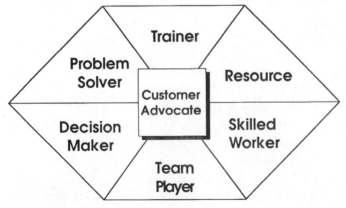

Figure 7: The Team Member Role

the general categories like trainer and resource with specific tasks and responsibilities.

- *Relate team member expectations to the team's overall purpose.* Discuss as a team how each team member can best contribute to team success.

- *Clarify responsibilities when action planning.* Each action item should have a team member assigned to it. Record these assignments on a written action plan.

- *Learn what others do on the team.* Create a plan for team members to learn about each other's roles and responsibilities. This could be as simple as a brief explanation of team member duties or as thorough as extensive cross-training and job rotation.

- *Figure out ways to help each other.* Learning each other's roles will enable team members to help out in other areas when needed. This builds a tremendous amount of flexibility and understanding between team members.

Open Communication

A collaborative environment in which there is trust and clearly defined roles cannot exist unless team members are committed to maintaining open and honest lines of communication. Effective team communication is more than being able to converse with one another. It means ensuring that important pieces of information are constantly being conveyed and understood by all team members. It also means that team members must be honest about their own wishes, needs, and concerns.

The following tips will be helpful for maintaining open communication on your team:

- *Err on the side of overcommunicating.* The inconvenience of sharing to much information is not as great as the potential risks associated with team members not having the information they need.

- *Seek to understand all angles.* This usually means soliciting input from team members and then listening with the intent to fully understand the intended meaning.

- *Take responsibility for being heard and understood.* All team members should work to get their message across so that its original meaning is understood.

- *Work to clear up misunderstandings quickly and accurately.* Misunderstanding, when left unchecked, can become the source of great contention among team members. It is usually best to clear up false information as soon as possible.

Reinforce and recognize team member efforts. Information sharing and soliciting input from others are activities that should be valued by the team.

Diversity

Differences exist because people have diverse styles and backgrounds. That diversity can lead to a very rich and rewarding team experience. People do not need to be the same or think the same to be unified. The key to team success is to value the differences on the team and utilize that diversity to achieve the team's common purpose.

The following tips will be helpful for valuing diversity on your team:

- *Remember that reasonable people can—and do—differ with each other.* No two people are the same. This does not mean one type is superior to the other. It is the diversity among team members that challenges the status quo and enhances creativity.

- *Try to learn as much as you can from others.* Learning the various backgrounds, cultures, and work methods of others can enrich your own skills and abilities while adding variety to your team experience. Team members may want to take turns presenting information in areas in which they have unique expertise.

- *Evaluate a new idea based on its merits.* Try to avoid evaluating ideas based on who submitted them or how closely they match your personal preferences.

- *Avoid comments and remarks that draw negative attention to a person's unique characteristics.* Humor is a key factor in a healthy team environment. However, humor should never occur at the expense of another's identity and self esteem.

- *Don't ignore the differences among team members.* Although team members should avoid derogatory comments toward individual differences, this does not mean that they should ignore the differences altogether. The differences should be celebrated and utilized to advance the goals of the team.

Balance of Task and Relationship

There are two basic types of needs or issues that arise on a team—task and relationship. Task issues relate to the actual work that the team must accomplish. Relationship issues relate to how well the people on the team get along and work together. A team that is too heavily focused on task may find itself overlooking important relationship issues. As a result, tension may rise and tempers may flare. A team that over-emphasizes relationships may find that important tasks do not get done or that quality begins to slip. As a result, the team may lose credibility as expectations are not met, motivation of team members may decline, and individuals may begin to point fingers.

The following tips will be helpful for balancing task and relationship on your team:

- *Regularly review and evaluate the effectiveness of team meetings.* Plan five to ten minutes at the end of each meeting to assess how things are going. What's going well that you want to maintain? What types of things does the team need to start doing more of? What types of things does the team need to stop doing?

- *Hold team celebrations for achieving results.* Celebrating success can be a great team-building activity. As your team reaches a major milestone, achieves a goal, or simply has a good month, take time to recognize your success.

- *Praise individual effort.* In addition to celebrating as a team, take time to recognize the efforts made by individuals.

- *Design individual performance goals that emphasize both results and teamwork.* Results achieved at the expense of team relations can have a negative effect. Likewise, teamwork without results can be just as debilitating.

- *Assign certain team members to monitor task needs and others to monitor relationship needs.* This may mean that one person is in charge of keeping the team informed on deadlines, action items, and goals. Another team member may be responsible for coordinating social activities on the team.

Resource 15. Managing Team Conflict

Although conflict usually involves a certain amount of struggle, if managed effectively, that struggle can be a source of strength and creativity. One thing is for sure—where there is a team there is bound to be conflict. It cannot be avoided.

There are numerous types of conflict in a team setting including:

- *Internal conflict.* An individual team member is experiencing a personal conflict that may or may not be related to the team. Nonetheless, the conflict is interfering with the person's ability to perform.
- *Individual conflict with one other team member.* An individual team member is experiencing conflict with one other team member.
- *Individual conflict with the entire team.* An individual team member is experiencing conflict with the entire team, or with several of the team's members.
- *Team conflict with one team member.* The entire team, or at least several team members, is experiencing conflict with one individual team member.
- *Conflict between several team members.* Several team members are experiencing conflict with several other team members.
- *Conflict between teams.* The team as a whole is experiencing conflict with another team.
- *Team conflict with one person outside of the team.* The team as a whole is experiencing conflict with one person outside the team.

Steps to Resolving Conflict

Responding to conflict in a timely and effective manner is the key to preventing it from disrupting the progress of the team. Regardless of the type of conflict you are facing, the same five-step process is helpful in resolving it:

Step 1. Acknowledge that the conflict exists. Although acknowledging conflict is not always easy, there is usually a sense of relief once the conflict is recognized. Teams are most effective when all team members share a commitment to individually recognize conflict situations and jointly work for solutions.

Step 2. Gain common ground. Put the conflict in perspective with the overall purpose and goals of the team. One way to assess the seriousness of any issue is to determine the extent to which the issue is getting in the way of team goals. If all members are committed to the team's goals, they should be willing to address issues that threaten the attainment.

Step 3. Seek to understand all angles. It is important to remember that gaining understanding does not mean gaining agreement. One need not agree to understand the point of view of another. The value associated with seeking to understand all angels have less to do with winning an argument than it does with gaining information.

Step 4. Attack the issue, not each other. Attacking the issue means that you are not at war with each other but with the conflict that is temporarily keeping you from progressing as a team. The goal is not to reach a win-lose solution, but to reach a solution that propels the goals of the team without violating the values of any one team member. Attacking issues side-by-side requires that you consider the other party to be a valuable partner in reaching a solution. Therefore, anger and hostility must be channeled into more productive activities such as problem solving and action planning.

Step 5. Develop an action plan. The final step in the process is to describe what each person will do to solve the problem. An action plan should be written so that each person can take accountability for their part in resolving it. Each person involved must fully understand the agreed-upon action steps.

Some common trip wires to avoid when attempting to resolve conflict include:

My Way or the Highway. Try to avoid placing your team or yourself in a situation that limits the alternatives, or forces people to choose between options and individuals.

Third-Party Decision.   At times it may be necessary to seek assistance from a manager or team facilitator. However, when we begin to depend on them to make our decisions and resolve all of our issues, we disempower the team. Teams should not automatically defer an issue to management simply because it is painful.

Under the Rug.   Because issues often run the risk of invoking emotion on the part of team members, it is tempting to simply sweep the problem under the rug and ignore that it ever existed. The problem with this approach is that the problems very seldom stay under the rug. They usually resurface later on in bigger and uglier forms.

Martyr Syndrome.   The martyr syndrome occurs when an individual gives in to the group or to another individual, but then acts as though they were the victim of group pressure. They may even try to use the fact that they gave in last time to get their way next time. Teams should work to avoid this type of behavior by constantly focusing on what is best for the team and not on whose turn it is to win an argument.

Parking Lot Commentary.   Parking lot commentary occurs when team members begin to talk about team issues outside the team setting. It is in such conversations that individuals vent the feelings that they were afraid to voice to the team. The problem with such behavior is that it undermines the trust and integrity of the team. Teams must work to ensure that all team members voice their concerns in team meetings. Individuals must refrain from saying things in the "parking lot" that they were not willing to say to the entire team.

Resource 16. Team Member Roles and Responsibilities

Clarifying team member roles and responsibilities is essential to a team just starting out, but can also be helpful whenever the team:

- Reorganizes
- Begins a new project
- Shifts individual responsibilities

- Sets new priorities
- Needs to renew commitment to team goals

Defining team member roles should promote shared responsibility. Defining team member roles is not intended to undermine the spirit of teamwork. It is intended to help all team members coordinate their efforts and maintain commitment to each other and to team results.

Some roles may require skills that team members do not presently have. This will require that the team either complete a learning plan or recruit someone from outside the team to fill that role.

In defining team member roles and responsibilities, the following steps are helpful:

Step 1. Analyze the work to be done. The first step to clarifying roles and responsibilities is to analyze exactly what type of work needs to be done. Doing so enables the team to define roles according to purpose and priorities and not personal preferences.

To conduct a work analysis, consider the following tips:

- *Review your team's charter.* This should include reviewing your team's purpose, priorities, and parameters.
- *As a team, discuss the key projects and activities that are necessary for accomplishing the team charter.* This discussion should include an evaluation of priority tasks, resources, responsibilities, and timeframes.
- *Identify team strengths and weaknesses.* Try to pin point what aspects of the team's work are going smoothly and in what areas the team is struggling.
- *Begin to organize the work into major areas of responsibility.* Make sure that the areas you establish are in alignment with the work process previously described. Avoid defining areas of responsibility based on personal preferences or traditional habits.
- *Identify team member strengths, talents, and expertise.* Begin to match team member strengths to key responsibility areas identified by the team.

Step 2. Define shared responsibilities. It is important to identify common responsibilities that all team members must fulfill.

Some tips to keep in mind when identifying basic team member responsibilities include:
- Reviewing team operating guidelines.

- Preparing your individual thoughts before discussing responsibilities as a team.
- Thinking of successful experiences where the team was able to function very effectively—what enabled the team to do so?
- Thinking of challenging times when the team has encountered breakdowns or conflicts—what got in the way and how could this be avoided in the future?

Step 3. Define individual roles and responsibilities. Defining specific roles and responsibilities for each team member enables you to learn how each person can contribute to team success and how team members can more effectively integrate their efforts.

Some tips for defining specific roles and responsibilities include:

- Considering the specific skills and expertise that are needed on the team given its purpose and priorities.
- Considering key projects and major areas of responsibility.
- Considering an individual's unique skills and strengths in relation to the purpose and priorities of the team.
- Involving the team's sponsoring manager to ensure clarity of team purpose and to add insight of individual roles.
- Preparing an individual role description for each person on the team.

Step 4. Learn each other's roles. With specific roles and responsibilities in place, it is time to create a plan for learning the roles of other team members. Even if you never intend to do what your team members do, knowing what they do can be extremely beneficial for a number of reasons.

Consider the following actions when learning each other roles:
- *Decide on the degree to which you must learn each other's roles.* This will depend on your team's need for specialization and integration.
- *Identify effective methods for learning each other's roles.* Once you know the extent to which you should learn each other's roles, you must identify effective methods for learning. In some cases, it might be appropriate to simply provide each other with role descriptions, in other cases, you may want to spend days working together.

- *Follow up on learning progress.* Periodically you should review the learning that has taken place and make adjustments as necessary.

Step 5. Review roles on a regular basis. It is important to review role descriptions periodically to ensure that they stay current and relevant to the team's overall purpose.

Tips for reviewing team member roles and responsibilities include:

- Setting a specific date (6 to 8 weeks out) to review roles and responsibilities in a team meeting.
- Looking for red flags that indicate the roles and responsibilities need to be reviewed.
- Being sure to stay knowledgeable on your own roles and responsibilities.
- Sticking to your plan to learn the roles of other team members.

Resource 17. Managing Team Performance

Gone are the days when managers alone could define performance expectations for workers. In today's business environment, it is crucial to focus on the expectations of key stakeholders. These expectations are what define acceptable performance for your team. Key stakeholders include customers, management, suppliers, peers, and team members.

Performance management in a team setting should focus on continuously striving to improve the team's ability to satisfy customers. Therefore, the process, although difficult at times, should be viewed as constructive and vital to the team's ongoing success.

Performance management is an ongoing process. Managing the performance of the team is not a once-a-year event where ratings are assigned. It is a day-to-day effort to maintain clear expectations, plan accordingly, take action, review results, and reward individual and team successes. Because it is an ongoing process, it is best managed by the people actually involved in doing the work.

Step 1. Define expectations. The first step to managing team performance is to make sure that expectations are clearly defined for the team as a whole and for individual team members. Many studies have shown that the primary source of performance problems is a lack of clearly understood and agreed-upon expectations. Think of your own work experiences. What frustrations result from not knowing what you are supposed to be doing, why it is important and what rules you must following in getting it done?

Steps to clarifying expectations include:

- Knowing your stakeholders.
- Defining your team's charter.
- Defining your key priorities.
- Knowing the team's key result areas, goals, and measurements.
- Defining parameters.

These expectations should be discussed and clarified with all team members.

Step 2. Planning. There are two important aspects to individual planning:

- *Results plan.* Focuses on what specific results must be achieved to meet expectations. This is done by setting measurable goals and action plans for each key result area.

In setting an individual results plan, the following steps are useful:

- Identify measurement method for each key result area.
- Measure current performance and establish a baseline.
- Determine a benchmark for what ideal performance would be.
- Set a realistic goal to move you toward the benchmark.
- Document goals.

- *Learning plan.* Focuses on the skills and knowledge that must be attained in order to achieve desired results.

In setting an individual learning plan, the following steps are useful:

- Review key result areas and performance goals.
- Determine what skills and knowledge are critical to success.
- Assess strengths and weaknesses based on critical skills and knowledge.

- Set development goals and capitalize on strengths and improve on weaknesses.
- Plan specific development activities for each development goal.
- Document your development goals and activities.

Step 3. Action. Plans are of little value unless action is taken. Action is what turns plans into reality. It is the action, or performance that we are trying to manage in the first place. It is important to remember to:

- Measure progress on a regular basis.
- Be Ready to correct poor performance. It is the responsibility of each team member to initiate corrective action as the need arises. Some helpful tips for correcting poor performance include:
- Recognizing that a performance problem exists.
- Analyzing the situation and determine root causes.
- Exploring possible solutions.
- Agreeing on a practical solution and create a realistic action plan.
- Implement solution by taking action and following through on commitments.
- Getting good help all along the way.

Step 4. Review. Teams should continuously track and discuss progress made toward key goals. This by itself is a form of review. Teams can use daily measurement charts and graphs to assist them. In addition, the team should take time periodically to more formally review results, gather feedback, review lessons learned, and set new courses of action for the future.

As the team reviews overall performance, the performance of individuals should also be reviewed. Team members can be a tremendous source of feedback for each other—especially when the focus is on making things better and not solely on what went wrong in the past.

Like planning, review should include two key elements: performance results (expectations met) and development progress (what skills and knowledge have been learned). When reviewing both performance and development, remember to look not only at results (what was accomplished) but also at the process (how you went about accomplishing the results).

Reward

Within your organization there are formal reward systems and informal reward systems. Teams can and should benefit from both these systems.

Formal reward systems are usually companywide. They are typically designed to attract and retain talented employees and to meet their basic needs. Two examples of formal reward systems are how people get paid, and what benefits they receive.

Informal rewards are usually tailored to specific teams and individuals. They are usually more personal, spontaneous, and flexible.

Both formal and informal rewards are essential to an effective organization. Although individual teams may not be able to easily change formal reward systems, they can directly impact informal rewards.

The following steps can be helpful in establishing appropriate rewards for your team:

1. *Understand your company's reward philosophy.* Learn the basic direction and objectives of your company's compensation process. You need not become an expert, but it is helpful to know your company's program so that you can work within it.

2. *Decide on what should be rewarded.* Determine as a team on what types of results and behaviors you would like to see rewarded both at the team level and at the individual level.

3. *Choose appropriate rewards.* Teams can and should play a big role in determining the types of rewards that are most meaningful to the members of the team.

4. *Deliver rewards.* Rewards should be given in a timely manner. Praise should be given to team members in public. Teams should have the opportunity to celebrate successes on a regular basis. Most importantly, rewards should be consistent.

Resource 18. Selecting Team Members

Selecting the right person to join your team is a critical decision that can have a long lasting impact on your success. The selection process presented here consists of six basic steps.

Each step helps to prepare the team for the next, thus leading to the selection of a successful team member. The steps should easily fit with the hiring procedures already in place within your organization.

The six steps are:

Step 1. Size up the work to be done. The first step to selecting a new team member is to analyze exactly what type of work needs to be done by the team and where a new team member is needed.

To size up the work to be done, consider the following tips:

- *Review your team's charter.* This should include reviewing your team's purpose, priorities, and parameters.
- *Discuss key projects and activities.* The team must review the tasks that are necessary for accomplishing the team charter. This discussion should include an evaluation of priorities, resources, responsibilities, and timeframes.
- *Identify team strengths and weaknesses.* Try to pin point what aspects of the team's work is going smoothly and in what areas the team is struggling.
- *Analyze and evaluate critical areas.* Look for ways to restructure what you are currently doing—this may include eliminating some work activities or reassigning who does what.
- *Develop a team learning plan to acquire new skills and knowledge.*
- *Define the role for the new team member.* The role description should be a result of the preceding analysis and should define the new person's overall purpose and responsibilities as a team member.

Step 2. Decide on selection criteria. To ensure that you consider all aspects of the new members role, selection criteria can be broken down into categories such as the following:

- *Technical skills.* What specific skills and expertise are we looking for?
- *General team skills.* What skills are expected of all team members in order to work effectively in the team environment?
- *Work qualities.* What attributes will enable the person to successfully contribute to team goals and projects?
- *Background.* What specific work experience will the successful candidate need to function successfully within the new role?

- *Education.* What specific degrees, certifications, or training will the successful candidate need to function successfully within the new role?

Step 3. Find possible candidates. Keep the following tips in mind when searching for possible candidates.

- *Develop a position description.* Position descriptions should briefly define the opportunity in terms of responsibilities, benefits, work conditions, and minimum qualifications. Make sure your description is honest and realistic. Be sure to include at the end of the description instructions on how interested candidates should reply.
- *Utilize search methods already established.* Most organizations have a process for posting job openings. That process can be quite helpful for describing the opportunity and getting the word out. Using the process may be necessary to ensure fairness and consistency. Be sure to check with your Human Resources representative.
- *Look in your immediate area first.* Often times you can find exactly what you are looking for right in your own area. Naturally, this will save you time and money.

Step 4. Evaluate candidates and make selection. To complete the evaluation process:

1. *Decide the evaluation methods.* As a team, decide how you will evaluate candidates against each criterion and who will be involved in doing the evaluating.
2. *Establish a method for tabulating and comparing results.* It is helpful to score each candidate on each criterion using a point scale. This allows you to compare the ratings each candidate received from each evaluator.
3. *Reach consensus as a team on your selection.* Your scores should provide an objective format for evaluating candidates.
4. *Discuss your decision with sponsoring manager.* As we mentioned earlier, selecting new team members requires constant communication with your sponsoring manager and Human Resources.

Step 5. Formulate the offer. Consider the following steps when extending an offer:

1. *Formulate the offer as a team.* When formulating the offer, it is helpful to include a few basic components. First, be sure to describe the new team member's role and responsibility. Second, explain what that person can expect as a

team member (this should include pay, benefits, resources, responsibility, etc.). Third, state how and by when the person should respond to your offer.

2. *Gain necessary approvals and assistance.* Involving your sponsoring manager and Human Resources is the key to this step. There are often certain policies and procedures that must be followed when discussing position offers.

3. *Extend the offer.* When the offer is made, it should include a date by which you would like the candidate to respond.

4. *Maintain a line of communication with the candidate.* Be sure the candidate knows who to call for answers to questions and to obtain additional information.

5. *Finalize the offer.* Once the offer is accepted, finalize the terms and establish a starting date. Work with your sponsoring manager and Human Resources to process all necessary paperwork associated with the new team member.

Step 6. Orient the new member. To successfully orient your new team member, consider the following tips:

- *Establish an orientation checklist.* The checklist should include all the steps the new member must take to become fully up-to-speed in the new position. The checklist should span from before the person's first day to at least one year out.
- *Decide who will be responsible for what.* Team members can be assigned to work with the new member on each item on the checklist.
- *Implement the checklist.* The entire team should work together to assure that each item on the checklist is accomplished.
- *Review progress on the checklist on a regular basis.* Such reviews help to provide necessary feedback and to ensure that all needs are met.

An effective orientation process should:

- Clarify the purpose priorities, and parameters of the team.
- Clarify the new team member's role and responsibilities.
- Clarify what the person can expect as a new team member.
- Provide training on team operations and guidelines.
- Introduce the new person to all team members and explain what they do.
- Define both individual and team performance objectives.

- Introduce the new member to key customers.
- Train the new member on critical skills and knowledge.
- Establish a long-term learning and development plan for the new member.

Resource 19. Team Leader Roles and Responsibilities

Not all supervisors or managers see the opportunities for them that accompany the transition to a team-based organization. The feeling of being "threatened" often stems from not having a clear idea of what the new requirements of their role will be in the team environment. Since supervisors and mangers have never performed many of the duties and responsibilities that they recognize will be required of them in the future, they naturally are apprehensive about taking the new assignment. In addition, high-involvement workplaces are often associated with flatter organization structures with far fewer levels of management than more traditionally structured organizations. This is often the case: Team-based organizations can sometimes operate with half as many management levels as their traditional counterparts. The reason is quite simple: By more effectively utilizing the intellectual and creative abilities of people at all levels in the organization, fewer people in the classical "supervisory role" are needed. This also poses a threat to many supervisors and managers—if their role is no longer needed, what will they do?

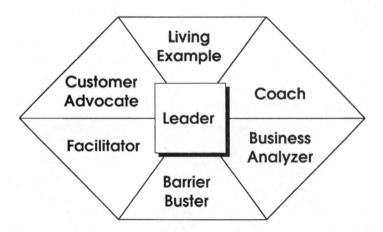

Figure 8: The Team Leader Role

The new role for managers and supervisors includes:

- Unleashing energy and enthusiasm by creating a motivating vision of a possible future and communicating group values and goals with tenacious consistency (leader).

- Being a role model of effective interpersonal communication, teamwork, and consistency between espoused values and daily actions (living example).

- Helping others develop to their fullest potential through training and personal support (coach).

- Understanding the environment surrounding the organization and developing strategy that takes advantage of business opportunities (business analyzer).

- Breaking down barriers that artificially limit the ability of the team to innovate and improve their performance (barrier buster).

- Providing the necessary resources, tools, and information to the team (facilitator).

- Working with customers and fully understanding their desires and expectations of the product or service (customer advocate).

Resource 20. Being a Living Example

There is no easy way to walk the talk. It requires a strong set of personal convictions, regular and open communication with others, and a continual awareness of how your actions are perceived. Some general guidelines that are helpful to remember include:

- *Being clear about what you stand for.* It is important to be very clear about what high performance means to you and what you see as its implications. When people are presented with the words "high performance team," numerous interpretations and corresponding expectations are created. It is important that you describe what it means to you—this will help align the expectations people have of your role in the change effort. It is also important that you are frank with your fears and apprehensions about the change. By setting an example early on that it is acceptable to be open and direct with concerns, others in the organization will be far more likely to share their feelings and reservations with you.

- *Understanding how others perceive your actions.* The adage, "Truth lies in the eye of the beholder," is apt. The fact is that how others perceive your actions determines, to a large extent, how willing they will be to support the changes you advocate. It is important to regularly solicit feedback from group members to develop an understanding of how you are being perceived.

- *Always looking for ways to demonstrate your convictions.* During the course of any given day there are numerous opportunities to demonstrate your convictions toward the creation of teams. Some of these opportunities are obvious, such as giving supportive comments during team meetings. Other opportunities are not so obvious, such as how much time you regularly spend talking with team members or how you react in a crisis situation.

From the perspective of the team, how you act in these informal settings is weighed just as heavily as how you act in formal ones.

As the team's leader, your actions are being continually evaluated and interpreted. It is important that group members receive the message that you are committed to the effort. Team members will be looking to see if the way you manage has truly changed. Among two of the most significant skills to develop during this transition are managing by principles rather than policies and utilizing boundary conditions rather than directives or edicts.

Managing by Principle

The practice of managing by principle stands in sharp contrast to the more traditional approach of managing by policy. Policies or specific rules and procedures are typically used as a means to assure there is some equity in decisions that affect people's work life. The resulting rule and procedure books help—at least that is the intent—to assure that people across the organization follow the same rules and regulations and are treated in the same manner. The problem of managing strictly by policies is that there are always exceptions—no policy can be perfectly written to take all the possible variables into account. The dedicated policy writer will continually add modifications to policies, ever enlarging the number of rules and regulations that need to be followed. This often serves to further complicate the process of using policies for making decisions.

A second problem with relying strictly on policy manuals is that they often remove the responsibility for making decisions. This sometimes leads to decisions that, from an outsider's perspective, simply do not make any sense.

Can organizations operate without policies? No. There are many rules and regulations that are dictated by law or contract agreements. Most organizations could, however, operate with far fewer policies and rules. The important ideas here is that only those policies that are absolutely critical should be specified.

So what is the alternative to managing by policy? We suggest that it is managing by principle. Some might argue that policies are merely principles translated into operational terms so they are clearer and more tangible. Our experience suggests this is often not the case. In fact, policies are sometimes in direct opposition to the espoused values of the organization. The reason is that policies are often created to deal with the exceptional rather than the majority of cases.

To use an analogy, principles can be thought of as the overriding umbrella that represents the ideals the organization is attempting to strive toward in much the same way the United States Constitution serves as the guiding set of principles for U.S. citizens. Within this broad framework there is certainly much room for interpretation—as seen by the numerous federal and state laws. But each law (analogous to organizational policies) is ultimately evaluated to determine if it is consistent with the principles espoused in the constitution—laws that are deemed unconstitutional are removed. The intent in managing by principle is to question all policies to assure they are consistent with the overriding principles of the organization. In doing this evaluation it typically becomes evident that the organization can operate with far fewer policies, rules, and procedures once the principles are clearly and widely understood.

To effectively manage by principles, there are four essential practices:

1. Assure everyone in the organization is clear what the guiding principles are.

2. Make the principles relevant—especially during strategy, problem-solving and decision-making meetings.

3. Work toward eliminating policies, procedures, and rules that are inconsistent with the operating principles.

4. Upgrade the operating principles over time.

Boundary Conditions

One of the key changes to the managerial role during the transition to high-performance practices is the shift from issuing directives to establishing boundary conditions.

Where a directive attempt to specify what needs to be done and how it should be accomplished, a boundary condition addresses only what the constraints or limitations are—the determination of what needs to be done and how it can best be accomplished is determined by the entire group rather than solely by the manager. To describe this dramatic shift toward utilizing boundary conditions, an analogy is useful. If we imagine that we are going to create a painting, boundary conditions might outline such things as what size the canvas needs to be and how much budget we have to spend on paints and brushes. We would then have the freedom to determine the subject matter, the colors that will be used to create the painting, and the best way to meet the budget. By contrast, directives are more like painting by numbers where all aspects of the job are carefully specified and the painter is merely following a process already outlined to them by someone else. There is little creativity, autonomy, or sense of ownership.

Boundary conditions help focus the group without unduly constraining them. They encourage the group to become creative in figuring out the best way to address the issue. Further, the group naturally has greater support for the decisions since they are directly involved in making them. This helps assure that the implementation of decisions is efficient and effective.

A manufacturing manager of a high-tech firm found himself trying to figure out the best way to transition a new product into the manufacturing area. Wanting to be consistent with his convictions around trying to create a more participative workplace, he decided he would define the boundary conditions he saw and then turn over responsibility to the group for deter-

mining the transition plan and developing the best floor lay-
out. In thinking through all the relevant constraints and limitations, the manager developed the following list of boundary
conditions:

- The work area can take up no more than 1500 square feet—
  there is simply no more available space in the facility.
- The new production line needs to be operable within four
  weeks—marketing has made commitments to customers that
  require a rapid start-up.
- The budget for the transition cannot exceed $10,000—given
  the current financial constraints within the organization,
  there is simply no more money available in the budget.
- The design of the line must be consistent with just-in-time
  and total quality practices—consistent with our manufacturing philosophy, we must strive to eliminate waste.

He presented the list to the production group. The reaction
was quite favorable. As one team member said, "The boundaries were realistic, clear, and gave us room to develop our own
design. I felt, for the first time in my career, that what I had to
say was going to really make a difference."

Resource 21. Barrier Busting

Most employees will report they face, on a daily basis, barriers
that inhibit their ability to make valuable contributions to
their company. Often this creates feelings of helplessness;
employees become frustrated at their inability to have an
impact on the future or direction of the organization.

In many ways, traditional management teaching and practice has actually encouraged the formation of barriers. The
very rhetoric of management is filled with ideas and approaches that tend to create barriers: "Isolate employees from
one another to minimize distractions"; "one person, one job";
"departmentalize" or "functionalize"; "inform on the need to
know"; "always follow the chain of command"; "do it by the
book"; "you're not paid to question the procedures, just follow
them." By contrast, managers and supervisors in team-based
work environments are expected to dismantle dysfunctional
barriers; in effect, to become "barrier busters."

The barriers that are created within organizations can be easily categorized into two groupings:

1. Those that were developed for legitimate management purposes and whose usefulness may (or may not) have ended.

2. Those barriers that are perceived to exist based on past practices or assumptions but, in fact, do not. The second grouping is the most intriguing for it suggests barriers that are not even real and often limit the contributions people make.

Since many barriers are merely perceived and have little or no foundation in fact, their dissolution is as easy as finding out what the facts really are.

Obviously, not all barriers teams encounter will be merely "perceived." Many barriers are legitimate policies, procedures, and structures that are well documented, widely understood, and regularly practiced. These rules and structures will almost certainly have been developed based on what was seen as being in the best interest of the business at one point in time—and it is quite possible that they are still legitimate practices by which to govern the majority of cases.

Whether one is trying to change a policy or improve the flow of information to the team, the steps we recommend for breaking down these "real" barriers follow the same path:

1. *Try to understand why the barrier exists in the first place.* What may seem as a barrier was probably first created with the best intentions. As a beginning step it is important to understand the genesis of the policy, procedure, or structure that has since become a barrier. The critical questions to answer are: What was the original intent of the policy/procedure/structure? What benefits did the company gain when this policy/procedure/structure was originally put into practice? In what ways is it still useful? (This last question is particularly important—it is possible that the policy/procedure/structure has not yet outlived its usefulness and therefore may not be worth your time and energy to try to change it.)

2. *Determine who you need to work with to eliminate the barrier.* At this point you want to identify a specific individual or specific individuals whose support you will need to overcome the barrier. The question to answer: Who can legitimately eliminate this barrier?

3. *Describe the consequences of the barrier on your team.* Since most managers respond favorably to measurable indicators, it

is preferable that these consequences are described, to the extent they can be, in "bottomline" terms. The question to answer is: What is the impact (measurable, if possible) of this barrier on the team's performance?

4. *Describe how to eliminate the negative impact of the barrier.* This is your plan of action for getting rid of the barrier. It should provide clarity regarding the specific steps that need to be taken to break down the barrier. The question to answer is: What specific changes must occur for this barrier to be eliminated?

5. *Identify the potential benefits and risks of the alternative you are recommending.* It is important to create a "realistic preview" of the potential benefits and potential pitfalls of the change you are advocating. If there are risks associated with the change, do not deny their existence—rather, affirm that you are aware of them and that you have thought through ways to minimize their potential impact. Key questions: What are the risks associated with eliminating this barrier? What are the benefits? In what ways can the risks be minimized?

6. *Identify opportunities to have your case heard.* Now that you have carefully thought through and prepared your case, you must get it heard by those who have the authority to make the necessary changes. This might mean setting up a formal meeting to present your ideas or it could mean taking advantage of an "accidental" encounter with an executive in the parking lot. Key question: How can I best get my case heard?

About the Authors

Belgard • Fisher • Rayner alliance companies serve organizations across North America, Western Europe, and Asia. Their clients include Ademco, Amdahl, Apple Computers, AT&T, Ball Aerospace, Compaq, Corning, Goodyear, Hanna Andersson, Hewlett-Packard, IBM Canada, Kemper, Marion Merrell Dow Inc., Martin Marietta Corp., McDonnell Douglas Corp., Monsanto Co., Motorola, MTV Networks, NBC, Port of Seattle, Rockwell International, Shell Oil Co., Taco Bell, Teccor Electronics, Travelers Insurance, Quaker Oats, Washington Water and Power, and Weyerhaeuser Co. All BFR efforts are focused on helping companies be successful when implementing high-performing organizations.

James Armstrong is a consultant, trainer, developer, and materials manager at BFR, Inc. He has a Masters of Organizational Psychology degree from the University of Oregon. Armstrong has worked in Tektronix, Hewlett-Packard, and Sequent Computer Systems prior to coming to BFR.

William Belgard is a co-founder of The Belgard Group. He has extensive consulting experience with Fortune 100 companies. He is co-author of a chapter of *Corporate Transformation: Revitalizing Organizations for a Competitive World* (Jossey-Bass, 1988) and *Helping Supervisors to Change* (with Janice Klein, Harvard University, 1991).

Kathy Braun is a principal with The Fisher Group. Prior to Fisher, Braun worked at Tektronix, Inc., managing advertising and media graphics and trade show conception, design, and delivery.

Barbara Brenneman is a high-performance work team member at The Belgard Group. In addition to materials distribution responsibilities, Brenneman has worked in customer service and general operations.

Mark Christensen is founder and president of Learning Point, Inc., a training and consulting firm specializing in management and work force development. As an associate at BFR, one of his most significant contributions has been as a primary author of the Team Tools™ series. Mark holds a master's degree in Business Administration from the University of Oregon.

Susanne Eaton is a co-founder of The Belgard Group. Eaton has extensive experience developing "people empowerment" in manufacturing, engineering, procurement and human resources organizations as a consultant and line manager. She has a liberal arts degree from the University of Oregon.

Kimball Fisher is a co-founder of The Fisher Group and author of *Leading Self-Directed Work Teams: A Guide to Developing New Team Leadership Skills* (McGraw-Hill, 1993). Fisher has published widely about team leadership. A former team leader at Procter & Gamble, Fisher has worked with a number of Fortune 100 companies implementing high involvement management practices across North America, Western Europe and Africa. He is a popular speaker at conferences on teams and organizational redesign.

Sheri Piercy is a high-performance team member at Belgard • Fisher • Rayner. Before working with the team at BFR, Sheri was in restaurant management for seven years.

Steven Rayner is the founder of Rayner and Associates and author of *Re-Creating the Workplace: The Pathway to High Performance Work Systems* (Oliver Wight Publishers, 1993) and *New Excellence: The Forest Grove Project* (Tektronix, 1984). Consultant, columnist, and training program developer, he has written more than a dozen articles on the subject of team-based organizations. Rayner regularly speaks on the subject of high-performance work systems, and he has consulted with companies implementing teams in the United States, Canada, and Europe.

Bonnie Sabel is a high-performance team member at BFR and works as BFR's accountant.

INTERESTED IN TEAM TRAINING PROGRAMS?

If you would like to receive additional information about the BFR alliance's training or consulting services, please mail or fax this form to us. Thank you.

I am interested in learning more about:

☐ BFR Team Tools®   ☐ The Course for Change Agents and Champions

☐ BFR Leader Skills™   ☐ Breaking Through/Breaking Out

☐ Personal Empowerment ☐ BFR Consulting Services

Name:		
Title:		
Company:		
Street address:		
City:	State:	Zip Code:
Country:		
Telephone:	Fax:	

Please send to any of the BFR Alliance Companies:

The Belgard Group Assoc.	*The Fisher Group*	*Rayner and*
1800 N.W. 169th Place	15075 S. W. Koll Prkwy.	5492 S. Harbor Ave.
Suite C600	Suite D	P.O. Box 1164
Beaverton, OR 97006	Beaverton, OR 97006	Freeland, WA 98249
TEL (800) 804-0660	TEL (800) 443-4447	TEL (206) 331-6773
FAX (503) 614-0856	FAX (503) 641-5235	FAX (206) 331-2047

We would like to hear from you about your team. Please let us know how these tips work for you or send us any additional tips you may have for dealing with the problems mentioned in this book. If you have other team problems you would like to get some tips about please contact us. We are happy to help.

The BFR Alliance Companies